KT-170-847

The
Jacobite
Cause

Prince Charles Edward Stewart's targe,
dress sword, and silver-hilted broadsword

The Jacobite Cause

BRUCE LENMAN

Richard Drew Publishing
in association with

 National Trust for Scotland

First published 1986 by
Richard Drew Publishing Ltd
6 Clairmont Gardens, Glasgow G3 7LW
Scotland

© Copyright 1986 Bruce Lenman

British Library Cataloguing in Publication Data

Lenman, Bruce
The Jacobite cause.
1. Jacobites
I. Title
941.07   DA813

ISBN 0-86267-159-0
ISBN 0-86267-158-2 Pbk

Cover Illustrations
Front: *Prince Charles Edward (from a portrait by Antonio David)*
             Glenfinnan Monument
Back: *Fyvie Castle*
             Monument at Culloden

Designed by James W. Murray

Set in Scantext Caslon by John Swain (Glasgow) Limited
Printed in Great Britain by Blantyre Printing and Binding Co. Ltd.

Contents

Colour Plates

An Exiled Dynasty and Its Ancient Kingdom

JACOBITISM IS A TERM DERIVED FROM THE LATIN WORD 'Jacobus' meaning James. As a political cause it was born late in 1688. Its adherents supported the main line of the Stuart dynasty as it strove to recover the thrones and dominions it lost as a result of the successful invasion of England in November 1688 by William of Orange. He was a Dutch prince who was the son-in-law of the monarch he overthrew and supplanted — James VII of Scotland and II of England, Ireland, and the overseas dominions of the English Crown. William's successful landing in England triggered off in that kingdom a sequence of events usually known to English historians as 'The Glorious Revolution'. The adjective 'glorious' was originally applied to the episode because it was bloodless. This was simply not true of events elsewhere in the realms of James VII and II. There was protracted and bitter fighting in Ireland. People lost their lives violently even in the province of New York across the Atlantic as the result of trouble produced by the Glorious Revolution in England. This was known as Leisler's Rebellion. In Scotland, the ancient kingdom of the Stuarts, there was a small-scale but spectacular and very violent civil war.

Despite the bitterness which flowed from these events, it is important to realise that they were to some extent a family squabble. William of Orange, who had been appointed Stadhouder in the republic of the United Provinces in 1672 when the Dutch faced invasion by France, was both the son and the husband of a Stuart. His mother was Mary, eldest daughter of the executed Charles I. His wife Mary was the eldest daughter of James VII and II by his first wife, the Protestant Anne Hyde. Mary and her sister Anne had been brought up Protestant at the insistence of James's elder brother and predecessor Charles II. Mary was heir presumptive to her father's thrones until June 1688 when James's second wife, the Roman

Catholic Italian princess Mary of Modena, gave birth to a boy chris-
tened James Francis Edward Stuart. This Prince of Wales was des-
tined for a long life, nearly all of which was spent in exile; he died in
1766. He is known to history by a variety of names: the Old Chevalier (from his use of the convenience-title Chevalier de St. George);
the Old Pretender (from the French word 'prétendant' which means
'claimant'); or 'James VIII and III' in the Jacobite succession. Had he
ever sat upon his father's thrones, there is reason to think that he
might have adorned them, for his was to be a sensible, moderate
temperament, much schooled in adversity. He never did occupy his
inheritance, although all the Jacobite rebellions of the eighteenth
century were raised in his name.

His very birth precipitated a major political crisis. Though James
VII and II had an unappealing public manner due to his rigid, and
deeply self-centred personality, he was not the monster of his foes'
propaganda. The first Whigs were in England a political movement
in the 1670s dedicated to excluding James from the succession on
the grounds of his Roman Catholic religion and absolutist politics.
Though they failed, they established a tradition of abuse carried on
by the Whigs who were the activists of the Glorious Revolution, and
by their successors in the eighteenth century. Before the birth of his
son, James's policies were essentially moderate, as they had to be if
he hoped to achieve his long-term objective which was the freeing
of his co-religionists from penal laws and their acceptance as fully
participating members of a society ruled by a Protestant. However,
James was a natural autocrat, and the prospect of a succession, of
Roman Catholic sovereigns greatly sharpened his passionate desire
for the re-Catholicising of his realms, by peaceful means, though
with all the patronage and persuasive power of the state behind the
campaign. Above all the massive expansion of his English army, and
his urgent desire to Catholicise its officer corps, gave his Protestant
subjects reason to believe that they had to act soon or they might
end up subjects of the sort of authoritarian, baroque, Counter-
Reformation, Catholic monarchy which they saw and disliked as the
normal form of government in Western and Central Europe. The
imperialism of James VII and II, a former Lord High Admiral of England, was entirely naval. His English army had no function to justify
its enlargement other than to hold down his subjects. It is just possible that by late 1688 James's more bigoted Protestant subjects
understood their monarch only too well. The fact that the English
upper classes, and above all the English nobility shared, for their
own reasons, the general unease, made the Glorious Revolution

possible: even in such a conservative society. William of Orange had been closely involved in English politics in the 1670s during the reign of Charles II. He had some measure of disguised involvement in the rebellion against James in 1685 in Scotland by Archibald, ninth Earl of Argyll. Argyll, the great chief of Clan Campbell, came back from exile to invade Scotland, starting with his native Argyll. Like the contemporary rebellion in the southwest of England led by Charles II's favourite bastard son, the Duke of Monmouth, the Argyll rising proved a failure. The ease with which he crushed both rebellions probably greatly encouraged James to go forward in that stubborn, inflexible manner which proved so fatal to him and which cracked open in something suspiciously like a nervous breakdown when he faced a real challenge in 1688. Like most politicians, James believed that the right of initiative was enough to permit a minority executive to ram unpopular policies through in the face of his resentful but apathetic peoples. Faced with a Dutch invasion and widespread defections from his camp, James who had been a brave soldier in his youth and a fire-eating Lord High Admiral as a mature man, panicked. He first sent the baby Price of Wales to Portsmouth into the charge of the loyalist Admiral Lord Dartmouth. William of Orange probably had little notion of supplanting James as King. Indeed, his political demands were initially perfectly compatible with the survival of James's kingship and the essentials of monarchy. James, however, was not prepared to compromise. He ordered Dartmouth to send the Prince of Wales to France. When his loyal admiral replied that he would die for the throne, but saw it no part of his duty to hand over the heir-apparent to France, James arranged for his son to take ship from Gravesend in late December in the care of the Queen, Mary of Modena. James himself tried to follow the next day, but his first attempt at flight was botched. Captured and returned, to the embarrassment of all, to Whitehall, he was allowed to flee again. As the English caroused at Christmas, James heard his first mass on French soil.

Since England was the core state of the Stuart state complex, its fate determined that of the rest. It was wealthier and much more powerful than any other province or kingdom in the British world, and its government had the determination to impose its will in the shape of a Protestant Succession on the rest. William and his wife Mary became joint sovereigns. Until the death of their successor Queen Anne in August 1714, Protestant Stuarts occupied thrones claimed by right by the exiled senior line of the family. Contempora ries, particularly propertied and privileged male contemporaries who owed their envied position as landed proprietors to the fact that they had inherited as eldest surviving sons, naturally found this exclusion of the Roman Catholic senior branch of the royal family both a relief and an embarrassment. Primogeniture was the basis of property right and the concept of hereditary right to the throne had been restored in 1660 at least partly because it was useful in keeping the lower orders submissive and deferential. One way out of the embarrassment was to produce the absurd tale that James Francis Edward Stuart was not the true son of James VII and II, but a 'supposititious child' smuggled into the palace in a warming pan. Babies were easily bought in seventeenth century slums, and heirs were indeed manufactured in this way on occasion, but this particular story was nonsense. The Prince of Wales looked like his father's son. Mary of Modena proved in exile that she, and James, were still fertile. Nobody who really mattered believed for a moment that there had been any substitution. Queen Anne ruled and died knowing perfectly well that 'the Pretender' was her half-brother. Even the exiled Stuart court nourished illusions that her conscience would make her try to atone for excluding him by arranging for his succession after her death. When she wanted to keep Jacobite pressure at a distance, Anne was not above surreptitiously encouraging such illusions. In the last analysis she was both tough and clear-minded. She knew who the Pretender was. She never intended him to have her job.

In Scotland, as elsewhere in the British world, there were very mixed reactions to the overthrow of James VII and II. However, it was only natural for the Scots to be more attached than most to a dynasty which was Scottish by origin and which had ruled Scotland since the accession of Robert II to the Scots throne in February 1371. Nor had the Scots developed in the later medieval period the bad English habit of changing kings and dynasties as the result of viciously-fought civil wars. The Stewart family, as the correct Scottish spelling of their name shows, were hereditary stewards of the Anglo-Norman royal court of early feudal Scotland. Inheriting through a lucky marriage, they occupied the throne century after century, changing the spelling of their name to Stuart in the sixteenth century when the French-speaking Mary Queen of Scots had difficulty with the letter 'w' which is not used in French. Her son James VI of Scotland succeeded to the English and Irish thrones in 1603.

Scotland had not seen a great deal of its kings after 1603. James VI and I promised to return regularly but, partly for financial reasons, visited his northern realm only in 1617. Charles I came a little more frequently. Charles II spent a brief uncongenial spell campaigning in Scotland in 1650-1, disliking both the country and its inhabitants so much that he was careful never to go there after the Restoration of 1660. Such neglect was not necessarily a bad thing. Scotland was, after 1603, quite the best governed of the three Stuart kingdoms because James allowed able and tactful men like Alexander Seaton Earl of Dunfermline to preside over the royal executive. The detailed attention which Charles I expended on Scottish affairs produced disastrous results, raising a major challenge to his authority from the bulk of the Scots aristocracy. Above all, the Restoration of 1660 was extremely acceptable to the Scots nobles. It was a restoration of the ancient kingdom from the toils of the Cromwellian Union of the British Isles. It was above all a restoration of the Scottish landed aristocracy, as well as of the old royal dynasty. The structure of the executive looked arbitrary on paper, but the implicit bargain was that the Scots aristocracy would actually run the government through its central organ, the Scots Privy Council, and that they would also be restored to their usual total dominance at regional and local levels.

Whereas the early modern state in England and Ireland grew out of a very centralised Norman-French feudal colony, the Scottish kingdom had never experienced such colonial status. It had absorbed rather than been overwhelmed by feudal influences with the result that they had reinforced the traditional decentralisation of Scottish society. The feudal barony was the basic court of first instance in Highlands and Lowlands alike. The office of justice of the peace had been introduced by James VI and I in deliberate imitation of English precedents, but it was only in the latter part of the eighteenth century that it became really important. In the late seventeenth century vast areas of Scotland were held as regalities, with rights of a royal nature in the hands of the proprietor. Regalities could be vast, or could be quite small areas like a town. The larger ones operated as petty kingdoms from which only cases of high treason went to the central Crown courts. Smaller ones operated more as hereditary sheriffdoms, but it must be added that many royal sheriffdoms had over time become hereditary in certain noble families. Thus on the Borders every single sheriff, the Crown's principal local officer in Scotland, was hereditary.

The Cromwellian regime which conquered Scotland in 1651 and ruled it until the Restoration of 1660 had deliberately set out to weaken the predominantly royalist Scottish nobles by abolishing heritable jurisdictions. At the Restoration those jurisdictions were all restored. The Stuarts ruled through and with the Scottish nobles. Many noblemen had become personally acquainted with King James when as Duke of York and Albany (the latter being his normal Scottish title), he had taken refuge in Scotland in 1679, at the height of agitation against him in England. He returned in the period 1680-82, acting as his brother's commissioner to the Scots parliament, and holding a viceregal court in Holyrood. That palace, part of which had been burned down by negligent Cromwellian soldiers in 1650, had recently been rebuilt and extended by a staunchly royalist architect, Sir William Bruce. Between 1671 and 1679 Bruce created a new front for the palace by building a replica of the existing James V tower and linking it with the original by a low balustraded screen and portico which, like the remodelled principal quadrangle, displayed a restrained classical style new to Scotland.

The politically prominent courtier nobles of the Restoration like John Drummond Earl of Perth and his brother Lord Melfort, respectively Chancellor and Secretary of State to James VII, were trendsetters for a nobility poor and proud. Nobles were also numerous. Scotland had as large a nobility as England, a country with more than four times its population. They presided over a conservative social hierarchy which left all serious political initiative in their hands. From the late thirteenth and fourteenth centuries the nobles and lairds had increasingly tended to live in tower houses, remarkable for their massive structure and a simple plan, usually involving several vaulted compartments set vertically, and further sub-divided by timber floors. The basic design was soon elaborated, but simple square tower houses based on a sequence of vaults went on being built as late as 1644, when Coxton tower house was built in this style in the Laigh of Moray. The tower house, in whatever form, became the supreme symbol of local power. In 1688 most members of the Scots aristocracy still lived in them, despite the introduction of classical architectural styles, derived from France and Italy, by Sir William Bruce.

Perhaps the most impressive flowering of the tower house tradition came in Mar, a province which in the sixteenth and seventeenth centuries was rich enough and stable enough to house its ruling class handsomely, whilst at the same time it was far enough from the heart of political power and strife to go its own way. Crathes Castle, built on a south-sloping site above the River Dee to replace an older tower surrounded in swamp in the Loch of Leys, was built from the late sixteenth century by the family of the Burnetts of Leys. Within a few miles of this fine structure stand two even finer ones. Castle

Sir William Bruce of Kinross, architect and Jacobite
(from a painting by Sir John Baptiste de Medina)

Fraser is the largest and grandest of these. Begun in 1588, it was externally largely completed by 1617, its main shape formed by a great central rectangular block with a projecting tower at either end, square on the north-west and a mighty drum shape on the south-east. It is, however, with Craigievar that this particular vernacular Scots style is generally thought to have reached its peak, combining an ingenious plan with great construction skill, and an architectural form of elegant ruggedness fashioning a slender shaft of tower from massive granite boulders covered by white-washed roughcast or harling. The fate of the Jacobite cause after 1688 in Scotland rested on the shoulders of the Scots aristocracy. Of course, they were divided over the issue, but Craigievar happens to illustrate some of the Restoration roots which later nourished the Jacobite rose.

Craigievar was first built by a family called Mortimer. In 1610 they sold it and the estate to 'Danzig Willie', William Forbes, an Aberdeen Baltic merchant risen to great wealth, not least by exporting woollen stockings and importing Baltic timber, tar, hemp and flax. Aberdeen was to be at one point a strongly Jacobite city. The older of its two universities, King's College, was not only devoted to the Stuarts, but the home of a very distinguished episcopalian theological tradition. Its ordinands often served as chaplains and tutors to the nobles and lairds of the North-East. Episcopalians formed the great majority of active Jacobites at all times, and 'Danzig Willie' was younger brother to the Bishop of Aberdeen. Here was a closely-knit, conservative regional society which linked noble, laird, and town merchant with ties of kinship and mutual dependence. It is no accident that the North-East gave much more active support to future Jacobite risings than any other part of Scotland. After 1688 its conservative local civilisation felt threatened by the new Whig-dominated political order, and it saw in the exiled dynasty a means of reversing trends it distrusted.

There was no way in which this sort of society was going to produce a social revolution forced through by the lower orders. The great majority of people were tenant farmers. In the numerous small burghs there were craftsmen, merchants, and a population of unskilled wage-earners. The richest merchants in an important burgh like Aberdeen would live in houses which were simplified versions of the more domestic style of laird's house which was becoming fashionable around 1600. Tolquhoun, built for William Forbes, 7th laird of Tolquhoun in Aberdeenshire, is a good example of this kind of structure and Aberdeen itself has two excellent examples of merchant's houses. Provost Ross's house in the Shiprow was actually built for one Alexander Farquhar in 1594, a century before Provost Ross became the householder. The other house of this type, which sits in the very heart of the modern city, is Provost Skene's House. Craigievar Castle shows that the social ambition of a successful merchant was normally directed towards entry into the landed classes. In a burgh like Montrose successful merchants needed landed estates for business purposes. Salmon was one of the main exports from the town, so control over fishing rights was important.

The towns or burghs of Scotland were divided into two groups. The more important ones, represented in the Convention of Royal Burghs, a meeting of delegates from town councils, were normally royal burghs by charter from the Crown, with certain exclusive rights to overseas trade in a landward area. Other burghs were burghs of barony, feudally dependent on an aristocratic master who administered them as an urban barony. Even the Convention of Royal Burghs usually accepted the lead of landed magnate politicians. The politics of burghs of barony directly reflected those of their noble masters. Thus Peterhead, a burgh of barony whose feudal superiors from 1593 to 1715 were the Keiths, hereditary Earls of Marischal of Scotland, followed the Keiths into active Jacobitism in 1715 and the town was forfeited and sold as a result.

There was really only one fully self-conscious class in early modern Scotland — the aristocracy. In that sense it was a one-class society because by manipulating dependence and deference the aristocracy could usually carry the rest of society with it. There were profound cleavages in Scottish society, but they were cultural and linguistic and not social. Of these by far the most important was the cleavage between the Anglo-Saxon Scots culture of the Lowlands and the Gaelic-speaking culture of the Highlands and Western Isles. The Northern Isles of Orkney and Shetland were a world apart by themselves, though even there national political developments could stir significant local responses. In Orkney, for example, an archipelago where a few officials of the Earl of Morton and a group of twenty or thirty lairds ruled over a population of some 23,000 people (nearly 2,000 of them in the Royal burgh of Kirkwall), Jacobitism became in 1745-46 a vehicle for the pursuit of long-established feuds within the ruling class. However, it was behind the Highland Line that the Jacobite cause found a far higher level of sustained support than anywhere else, and it is important to be clear about the distinctive aspects of Gaelic society in Scotland.

Though we lack reliable overall figures, it is clear that a much higher proportion of Scotland's population lived behind the Highland line around 1700 than at present. In 1755 the total population of Scotland was estimated at a million and a quarter, of which perhaps 400,000 lived in a broadly defined Highlands and Western

Islands. The population history of the Highlands did not differ significantly from that of the Lowlands in the seventeenth century. People intermittently starved or died of disease in the seventeenth century in both the Highlands and the Lowlands. The period 1695-99 was especially grim. However, as long as Highland population stayed below the maximum which could be fed from usable land in average years by contemporary agricultural techniques, there was no recognised problem. The early eighteenth century may have seen some population growth in the region, partially sustained by the introduction of the potato after 1740, when it was first cultivated in the Outer Hebrides. On the other hand, by this date there were already the first faint signs that population was pressing the limits of the region's capacity to feed and gainfully employ it. Black cattle were the main export from the Highland region. Because they could feed on land too poor for crops, they were an ideal surplus to exchange for grain to cope with the endemic regional grain deficiency, but the better-organised cattle farming was, the fewer people it needed to operate it.

Highlanders were distinctive by reason of language and social custom. They very often, but not invariably, also wore a distinctive form of dress. A woollen bonnet was common to the lower orders in both Lowlands and Highlands. Judging by clothing preserved in and recovered from bogs, Hebridean peasants could wear stockings, breeches and a jacket like Lowland peasants, but they also wore the kilted tartan plaid over their shirts. At least up to the early part of the eighteenth century this garment was the size of a small blanket. It was carefully folded on the ground. The wearer rolled himself into it, fastening the lower part round his waist with a belt and draping the rest over his shoulders. The whole subject of tartan and the evolution of the small kilt is contentious, but John Telfer Dunbar does seem to have said all that needs to be said on both topics in a book published in 1962. There may have been regional patterns in tartan weaving, but there was absolutely no consistency in general usage. Clans were distinguished by cap badges, not by distinctive tartans, which are mostly a Victorian development, and a sign of living vitality in distinctive Scottish dress. The small kilt or philabeg evolved naturally in the early eighteenth century, from the lower part of the belted plaid. For riding, Highland gentry wore tight tartan trousers or trews.

The Gaelic tongue of the Highlander set him radically apart from his Lowland fellow-countryman. This ancient, Indo-European Celtic language was not easy to acquire in an age when many of its

1. *James Francis Edward Stewart, the Old Pretender, as a boy*
   (from a painting by François de Troy, 1701)

2. The Old Pretender as a man (by an unknown artist)

17th-century peasant costume.
The clothing mounted on these models was recently recovered
from peat bogs in Northern Scotland

speakers were still monoglots. Nor was its literary tradition easy of access. Of great antiquity, it was expressed in complicated poetic metres and an archaic literary language which looked back to Old Irish. Only in the seventeenth century did Scots Gaelic begin to break away from a shared Scoto-Irish cultural world, and its written forms remained in the custody of trained specialists, usually bards retained by chiefly families. By the eighteenth century, the upper classes of the Highlands and Islands were bilingual in Gaelic and English. Every single chief could speak English. For some it was already the preferred domestic language.

James, third Duke of Perth and an ardent Jacobite, once sent two sets of Highland dress to the exiled Stuart court in Rome, as presents for Prince Charles and his brother Prince Henry, the sons of 'James VIII and III', the Old Pretender. After the '45 the British government tried to stamp out distinctive Highland garb, less for its own sake than as a symbol of a social system it wished to destroy. Highland clans were regarded by eighteenth-century Lowlanders and Englishmen as at best an anachronism, and at worst a menace. They were certainly unusual, with no exact parallels, even in Gaelic Ireland. Unfortunately scholarship teaches us that every clan was different, so all generalisations break down. Nevertheless generalisation is unavoidable.

Most clans were based on a fusion of feudal and tribal principles. Very great Highland magnates like the Dukes of Atholl relied mainly on landownership and jurisdictional authority of a kingly kind in the huge Regality of Atholl. Tribal loyalty was relatively unimportant to them. They were exceptional. Most Highland chiefs carefully cultivated, or rewarded bards for cultivating, a sense of clan identity formed round a common surname and a common descent from some remote ancestor. The great bulk of clansmen cannot possibly have had a blood tie with their chief. Quite a few chiefs, like the Fraser, Rose, and possibly Cameron chiefs were of Norman origin. The Campbell chiefs were of ancient British stock from the pre-Gaelic world of the Kingdom of Strathclyde. The tribal spirit, which made of the reigning chief the father of his people, was nevertheless most important when combined with landownership and feudal jurisdiction at the level of at least a barony. Landownership and feudal law disciplined a clan. Groups like the MacGregors who had group identity without land, jurisdiction, or an accepted chief, were simply pariahs in this world, and for most of the Jacobite period were subject to penal laws which tried to destroy their very name.

Power and prestige spread down in a clan from the landlord chief, in the first instance to subordinate gentry called tacksmen. In many ways they were the clan. They usually were descended from the chiefly house. These collateral branches holding tacks (the Scots word for lease) on reasonable terms, would sub-let land to the mass of the peasantry. These poor clansmen, holding by a precarious tenure, were farmers, living usually in scattered hamlets or clachans, and farming by archaic methods arable divided in scattered strips on the 'run rig' principle, and pasture held in common beyond the head dyke which protected the arable from stock. Tacksmen were lieutenants in the clan army. This was still an Iron-Age warrior society, a shame-and-honour society where rent was in fighting men. Here were potential soldiers for the exiled dynasty.

CHAPTER II

Claverhouse
and the
First Jacobite Rising

BY 1688 THE REGIME OF JAMES VII IN SCOTLAND HAD
become an unpopular clique, mainly by the systematic alienation of
the great bulk of its own conservative supporters. The small groups
of religious activists of a Presbyterian persuasion who had challenged Stuart authority intermittently since 1660 were probably
more of a help than a hindrance to the dynasty. They are often
referred to as Covenanters, for they looked back to the National
Covenant and the Solemn League and Covenant, drawn up by
opponents of the government of Charles I. However, the Covenanters of the late 1630s and early 1640s were the social élite of contemporary Scotland, in alliance with some of the ablest ministers of the
Kirk by Law Established. The Covenanters of the early 1680s were
tiny cliques of radicals, still capable of appealing widely to the lower
orders of society when given the chance, but by 1684 dispersed and
hunted through the bogs and moors of their strongholds in the
south-west of Scotland. Their indomitable defiance of royal authority merely confirmed the view of the propertied and privileged that
the dynasty was an essential bulwark against radicalism and social
upheaval. The radicals' uncompromising Presbyterianism probably
went far to reconcile the nobility and gentry to that urbane blend of
Presbyterian underpinnings and Episcopal leadership which was
the Church of Scotland of the Restoration. Its crippling subordina-
tion to the state only became a lethal handicap under a Roman
Catholic sovereign.

James, however, carried his policies in Scotland through with a
high hand, and with tarnished subordinates. His leading servants
came under heavy pressure to convert to Catholicism. Some, like
Lord Perth, did so in all sincerity. Like his royal master, Perth was
essentially a very conservative man, deeply disturbed by the intellec-
tual and social trends of the period. Like the great contemporary

English poet John Dryden, Perth was a disturbed and in many ways sceptical conservative who saw in the authority of Rome a bulwark of prescriptive right. Yet, other Stuart henchmen, like Perth's brother Melfort, experienced conversions of so blatantly political a nature as to enhance the reputation of neither themselves nor the regime. Sir Robert Sibbald, Lord Perth's doctor, appears to have converted mainly to get Perth off his back, and he not unreasonably reversed the process after 1688, when his patron ceased to be in a position to badger him about religion. The simple fact was that the bulk of conservative Scotsmen saw no need to adopt the dramatic measures of their monarch, Perth, or Dryden. They were firmly in the saddle at local level and increasingly the most radical threat facing them seemed to be the interfering and unseemly policies whereby the Crown tried to push measures which commanded no general support.

For example, autonomy of the burghs had been a pillar of Scots monarchy since the early medieval period. In a constructive partnership, the royal burghs administered themselves whilst cooperating with and contributing financially towards royal government. To ensure that his policy of religious toleration for Dissenters and above all Roman Catholics was implemented, and that towns did not obstruct his measures, James began to impose direct rule on quite important burghs. Dundee, a staunchly royalist place, found General John Graham of Claverhouse, Viscount Dundee, nominated as its Provost. He happened to be the heir to the much-resented claims of the medieval Constable of Dundee to control certain aspects of burgh government. He was also a local laird, with castles at Claypotts to the east of Dundee, and Dudhope on its northern boundary. The burghers, even before he became their mandatory Provost, must have looked at him with the same ambiguous feelings they reserved for the Hilltown, the 'free' suburb which climbed the slopes of the Law Hill and tried to use their markets without paying their stent or tax. Of course, it hardly mattered that a mere burgh sulked, but the desertion of the Privy Council by most of the magnates, and the bitter feeling in the Established Kirk that it was being sold down the river because it could not put effective pressure on the Crown, meant that James had little positive support left in Scotland when he made the mistake of moving the bulk of his small Scottish army into England to help deal with the Dutch invasion. Even those of an Episcopal persuasion in Scotland welcomed the news of the enterprise of the Prince of Orange, for they had no idea that James would simply cut and run. They expected him to have to negotiate, without the privilege of refusing any modification of his policy.

The Glorious Revolution in England effectively destroyed the existing Scottish administration, but as in England it was the behaviour of King James which forced the Revolution into radical courses. By March 1689 a Convention Parliament had called itself into being in Edinburgh. It was obvious that committed Williamites or supporters of James, who were beginning to be called Jacobites, were not in a position to control it. The balance lay with a large block of 'dontknows'. On 16 March 1689 letters to the Convention from both William and James were read. That of William was an exercise in aimiable generalisation. The one from James destroyed his own cause. It was an aggressive reassertion of the view that he had an absolute right to the 'natural allegiance' of every Scot, combined with violent threats against all who failed to obey him. Conservatives were left paralysed by the implications of this doctrine, and on 4 April 1689 a virtually unanimous Convention resolved that James VII had forfeited the Crown of Scotland. The nobility were, like James, the product of primogeniture but they were numerous enough to have a range of abilities in their ranks. Some were shrewd and many sensible. They had a natural tendency towards the average, the acceptable, the practical. Only a handful of committed Jacobites stood out, under the leadership of Viscount Dundee, who himself recognised the hopelessness of his political position. After conferring with his fellow Jacobite George, fourth Duke of Gordon, who commanded Edinburgh Castle, Dundee rode out of Edinburgh north to his estates around Dundee.

As he did not recognise the government of the Parliament or Estates of Scotland, conflict was inevitable. His kinsman the great Marquis of Montrose had devastated Scotland in the 1640s with an army whose core was composed of Roman Catholic troops from Ulster. Civil war was raging in Ireland in 1689. The Estates knew Claverhouse still had with him some of the professional cavalry soldiers of King James. They had to insist that he recognise them or fight. In April 1689 Dundee raised the standard of King James on Dundee Law. The first Jacobite rebellion against the *de facto* government of Scotland had begun.

It was to be an inspiration to all future Jacobite rebellions, not least in the sacrificial death of its leader in the hour of victory. Nevertheless, the really decisive feature of this rising was the poor showing it made in terms of attracting active support. After all, King James had run a Scottish political system supported by the great

Claypots Castle, Broughty Ferry,
a late example of the tower house. It once belonged to
the Jacobite John Graham, Viscount Dundee

bulk of the nobility and gentry. It had been possible for much of the reign of Charles II to dispense with the services of any significant force of professional soldiers, because the county militias led by the aristocracy were ready and willing to deal with external foes, and internal subversion. Now in the spring of 1689 even the burgh of Dundee closed its gates on the Jacobite general. He burned the Hill-town, presumably to the great delight of the Dundonians, who dis-liked it, and he then moved into the Highlands to fight a war of man-oeuvre.

We know a great deal about the campaign which followed, not least because it became the subject of the last major Latin epic written in Scotland, 'The Grameid' which was written by Dundee's standard-bearer James Philip or Philp of Almerieclose. Against Dundee the government of the Estates sent an army commanded by a Highlander, Major-General Hugh Mackay of Scourie. He had spent a lot of his life in the Netherlands, was married to a Dutch wife, and indeed commanded some Dutch troops in this campaign. There had long been a Scots Brigade in the Dutch service and it played a significant role in the Glorious Revolution. Dundee's forces were a motley collection. By far the most important point about them was that apart from Cameron of Lochiel they included not one major Highland or Lowland magnate. Former pillars of the Stuart regime like the Earl of Strathmore did not embrace the Williamite cause. Nor did they fight for King James. They sulked at home.

Dundee did manage to pull a couple of thousand men together in the Highlands by May of 1689. Some came from marginal groups who could be relied upon to join any good rebellion. Coll MacDonald of Keppoch, notorious as 'Coll of the Cows' for his cattle-thieving, came with his fierce little clan. His territory was so remote that his home base was deemed virtually immune to regular troops. His last battle had involved fighting the troops of James VII. He fought bravely under Dundee. Far more committed were the MacGregors, who had been allowed the use of their clan name again in 1660, for loyalty to the Stuarts in the Cromwellian era, and who lost it again for their behaviour in 1689. The penal laws were reimposed in 1693. Small western clans like the MacDonalds or MacIains of Glencoe, from the fringes of the fallen Campbell empire, also rallied to the Jacobite standard. The MacDonalds of Clanranald formed part of Dundee's force as did their kinsmen of Sleat. The different branches of the Clan Donald had long acted as distinct clans. Sir John Maclean of Duart, a young chief also precariously placed on the frontier of Campbell expansion in Mull, was to the fore, as was the venerable Sir Ewen Cameron of Lochiel, a very important Highland magnate indeed and a gallant warrior, albeit one whose violent protestations of loyalty in the Restoration era had owed something to the need to bury the memory of his sensible accommodation with the Cromwellians in the late 1650s.

The strategic pivot of the campaign was Blair Castle, the seat (though not the usual residence) of the mighty house of Atholl. The family usually lived in a more accessible home in Dunkeld, but Blair held a key position blocking the Garry-Tay valley through the Central Highlands and also controlling the very important route by Glen Tilt to the upper reaches of the Dee valley, and the North-East. It was very much the military crossroads of the Grampian Mountains. Atholl himself had been a staunch supporter of King James against Argyll's 1685 rebellion. John, second Earl of Atholl was about as committed a Restoration royalist as could be found. He had fought in Glencairn's rising against the Cromwellian regime in Scotland in 1653-4. He fought against radical Presbyterians at the battles of the Pentland Hills in 1666 and Bothwell Brig in 1679. A colonel of militia, he participated in the misleadingly-named 'Highland Host' sent on a punitive operation to daunt the Whigs of the West of Scotland in 1678. He was the principal officer in the operations against Argyll's rebellion in 1685, and his Atholl men helped occupy Argyll. Mackay, the Williamite commander in 1689, was worried that there might well be incidents between the Argyll men in his ranks and the people of the Atholl countryside, due to the bad feeling engendered by the occupation. In February 1673 Atholl's loyalism was rewarded by a patent as Marquess of Atholl, Earl of Tullibardine, Viscount Balquhidder and Lord Murray, Balvenie and Gask. James VII made him one of the original Knights of the Thistle in 1687. At the time of the crisis of 1688-9 he was in Bath, the English spa, 'pumping his head'. His position was ambiguous. He was briefly held in custody in London in August 1689, by the Williamite government, but that such a man should be ambiguous is a measure of the dynasty's peril.

His eldest son John, Earl of Tullibardine, from May 1703 second Marquess and from June 1703 first Duke of Atholl, was left in charge of the estates in 1689 and was a mild but unquestioned Whig. The Jacobite tradition was upheld by the family steward, Stewart of Ballechin, who had commanded the occupying garrison at Inveraray in the winter of 1685-6, and who in 1689 seized and held Blair Castle for King James, despite notably feeble efforts to frustrate him on the part of the heir, Tullibardine. Dundee moved towards Blair. Mackay marched his forces up the Tay towards the same objective. It was a classic recipe for a battle. Dundee chose to fight Mackay before he could reach and take Blair. As Mackay and his men emerged from the narrower parts of the Pass of Killiecrankie, just a few miles from Blair, they realised that the small Jacobite army of about 2,500 men was stationed on hillsides to the east. A general action ensued.

The military potential of a Highland army was not fully appreciated by the orthodox regular soldier of the day. That is hardly surprising. Highland weapons, organisation and tactics were all in a state of some fluidity. The classic weapons of Highland war until the end of the fifteenth century were the two-handed sword or claymore, and the bow and arrows. The claymore was a fearsome wea-

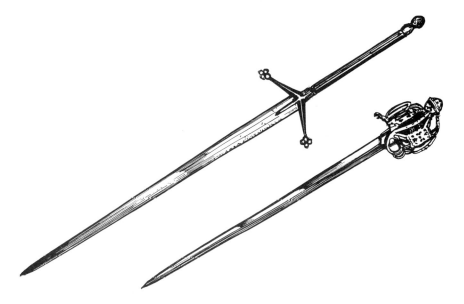

The old and the new in Highland swords, a 16th-century claymore and the basket-hilted broadsword of the Jacobite risings

pon. It was a hand-and-a-half length (slightly smaller, in other words, than the contemporary Continental two-handed sword). The guard was of diamond section sharply angled into the blade. Another distinctive Scottish feature was the way the guard terminated in quatrefoils built up by brazing iron circles together. It was the classic weapon of the many Scottish mercenaries in sixteenth-century Ireland. The drawback of the weapon was that it could not be carried with a shield. Body armour was necessary, and by the seventeenth century armour was not proof against bullets. Killiecrankie was won by men wielding lighter weapons.

The bulk of the 2,500 Jacobite fighters at Killiecrankie were lightly-armed infantry. Dundee, in his silver and buff coat set off by a green scarf, sat in the middle of his line of battle, surrounded by his small troop of horse. The Highlanders massed on each of his wings had thrown off their heavy belted plaids and had prepared themselves for action by knotting their shirt tails between their thighs. Barefooted and bonneted, they were armed with a light round shield or targe of oak and hide studded with brass, and a basket-hilted broadsword. Seventeenth century blades are invariably two-edged

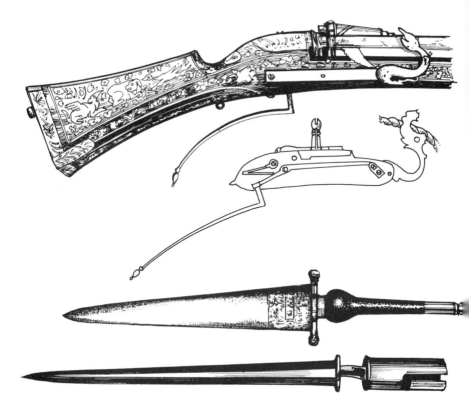

A matchlock musket with an example of both plug and socket bayonets

(eighteenth century usage was more varied and included many single-edged blades known as backswords). The blades were often of German origin, but the basket guard was a very Scottish feature and earned the completed weapon the common name of a 'Highland sword'. A metal spike could be screwed into the middle of the targe and the targe hand could also carry the big Highland stabbing dagger known as a dirk. We know from the 'Grameid' that a mixture of other weapons were carried by the Jacobites, ranging from two-handed axes to blunderbusses. Muskets there certainly were in some Jacobite hands, but they saw little use.

With his back to the River Garry, Mackay extended his infantry line. His men were equipped with the usual mixture of weapons ranging from old-fashioned matchlocks fired by using a smouldering cord and capable of a rate of discharge of only one round a minute, to more modern flintlock muskets, more accurate and with double the rate of fire, but by no means standard issue. As late as 1697 two soldiers in William's army carried the matchlock for every three with the new musket. Mackay's cavalry was in no position to charge uphill, and he seems to have had no effective field artillery. His men had the clumsy plug bayonet of the period which was secured by pushing its tapering handle into the muzzle of the musket. Musket fire was most inaccurate beyond about 60 yards range. Plug bayonets were slow to fix and ruled out another round.

As Mackay stretched his line to avoid being outflanked he ended up with a very thin line facing two clumps of Jacobite infantry, for Dundee hardly needed a centre. For two hours on that fatal 27 July 1689, the rival forces stared at one another, no comfortable experience for green troops, which is what the bulk of those present on both sides were. Then, with the sun no longer in his army's eyes at 7 p.m. Dundee ordered a charge. Mackay's line delivered one volley, which felled 900 or so of the attackers, but the Williamite line then disintegrated as its troops, fumbling with their bayonets, were swamped by a mass of swordsmen, active as monkeys and moving very fast. It was all over in about three minutes, though the pursuit of the broken line was sustained and murderous. Safety lay in standing firm. The gallant Mackay rallied some Dutch and other troops and retreated with this remnant across the Garry fords. Dundee, charging with his few horse, fell dead to a musket shot in his moment of glory.

Mackay summed it all up later with grim precision:
'The Highlanders are of such quick motion that if a Battalion keep up its fire until they be near to make sure of them [i.e. of hitting them], they are upon it before our men can come to the second defence, which is the bayonet in the musle of the musket.'
He knew he had left 2,000 dead or wounded, or captured men at Killiecrankie, full half his force, but he had only lost a battle, not the war. War is a hard pounding with victory to the side which endures best. The Jacobite army still had to break into the Lowlands to make any political impact. Its obvious path was by way of Dunkeld, a trading town situated in a natural gap where the Tay punches through friable slate rock formations.

In Dunkeld Dundee's incompetent successor Colonel Alexander Cannon met his nemesis in the shape of a regiment formed from the ranks of former militant Presbyterian opponents of the Stuarts. It was associated with the Earl of Angus and its young lieutenant-

Dunkeld, the small town which saw vicious street-fighting in 1689, now beautifully restored by the National Trust for Scotland

colonel was William Cleland. Known as the Cameronians after one of the strictest of the Presbyterian sects, this highly motivated infantry unit had barricaded itself into the little town which clustered round the partially-ruined medieval cathedral. Built to receive some of the relics of Saint Columba, whose cult was part of the cultural imperialism of the royal house of Canmore but which never succeeded in supplanting the far older eastern cult of St Andrew, Dunkeld Cathedral had always been far too large for the community around it. Maintained in the usual medieval way by bleeding the revenue of country parishes, it had very sensibly been cut down to the scale of a parish kirk after the Reformation. The chancel and choir thus remained in use. The nave was left an impressive ruin. Around the cathedral lay the complex of charming vernacular houses which had formed the cannon's manses and an important market site. Restored by the National Trust for Scotland, they still give an impression of the harled domestic architecture, with its craw-step gables and gardens sloping down to the Tay, which was the early modern burgh.

For the Highland army it proved a trap. The Cameronians held the mansion of the Marquis of Atholl and sallied out to set fire to any houses from which the Highlanders tried to maintain a steady fire. For four hours on 21 August 1690 the street fighting raged until the Jacobites recoiled, mauled and baffled. Like Dundee, Cleland fell in his hour of victory. Important figures like the elderly Lochiel had already returned home (though many of his Camerons remained in the Jacobite ranks), Cannon retired back into Lochaber for the winter. Any chance of reviving the flagging Jacobite cause now rested almost entirely on massive reinforcement from Ireland or France.

It was not to be. The Jacobite cause was not high enough on French military priority lists, and in Ireland, despite the presence of King James, the current of military events was beginning to run in favour of the Williamites. James only ever sent a handful of poor-quality Irish troops to reinforce his disappointingly small band of active Scottish supporters. Early in 1690 he did send Major-General Thomas Buchan to try to revitalise the Jacobite army. Mackay bestirred himself as spring came to the Highlands. On May Day 1690 his cavalry caught Buchan's force at the Haughs of Cromdale, a low-lying flood plain beside the Spey, and rode over their unprepared enemies. It was a rout so total that a later Jacobite ballad had to call in the ghost of the long-dead Marquis of Montrose to reverse the true verdict. Ironically, that royalist martyr had himself been routed in a manner very similar to Buchan, in 1645 at the Border battle of Philiphaugh. The military challenge to the Revolution in Scotland was dead by the early spring of 1690. It had only briefly looked serious. There was little positive support for King James, even in the ancient kingdom of his dynasty. That was hardly surprising — the man had displayed political ineptitude of almost heroic proportions. In the end, he had abandoned his two British kingdoms rather than compromise.

CHAPTER III

The Growth of Jacobite Sentiment 1690-1708

THERE WAS A PALPABLY FALSE CONTEMPORARY theory that King James had abdicated when he threw the Great Seal of England into the Thames during his second and successful escape bid. James should have known what he intended, and he said the gesture was an attempt to paralyse the new regime, which he regarded as a clique of rebels and heretics. However, it must be stressed that the man who removed the senior line of the Stuarts from the British thrones was James VII and II. There was not a breath of serious republican sentiment, despite the fact that a republican Commonwealth was within the memory of many living Englishmen. James could have stayed. William would never have dared claim the throne, and the Prince of Wales would undoubtedly have succeeded to his inheritance, though of course he would have been brought up Protestant. After the failure of his Irish campaign at the Battle of the Boyne, James returned to France. He preferred exile to having his powers curtailed. He had a brief resurgence of hope in June 1690 when in a naval battle off Beachy Head the English and Dutch lost the mastery of the Channel to the French fleet. Even Louis XIV, often curiously obtuse in matters naval, could see the opportunity for an invasion of England, but his troop concentrations were delayed intolerably by military pressures on his land borders, and by the time an invasion force was available, the Anglo-Dutch fleet had been built up to a point of clear superiority, which it underlined by a smashing defeat of the French Admiral Tourville at the battle of La Hogue early in 1692.

Firm conservative government in Scotland might have sufficed to bury the Jacobite problem. Regrettably, that was precisely what the new regime in Scotland found it could not provide. Partly, this was for reasons beyond its control. The Church of Scotland had under the Restoration been very much to the taste of the more conservative of the aristocracy, particularly in the northern parts of the kingdom, where little radical religious dissent existed. Bishops were seen as a guarantee of order and seemliness, but they were warned that they must not in any way challenge the political and social ascendancy of the nobles. Lay patronage ensured that parish ministers were in general on good terms with their noble patrons. In the Netherlands, where he was surrounded by radical exiles of a Presbyterian persuasion, William had not grasped the depth of Scottish upper-class commitment to bishops, but as the Scots nobles flocked to him in London, he rapidly learned the true state of affairs. Committed Calvinist though he was, William liked the element of royal control in an Episcopal system (and in any case even Calvin himself had been prepared to countenance bishops as appropriate under certain circumstances). Bishops might have survived but for a disastrous interview between William and Bishop Rose of Edinburgh which left William convinced of the stubborn Jacobitism of the episcopal bench. There was no alternative to a Presbyterian settlement in the Kirk and by 1690 it was accomplished.

The most important single figure in the new establishment in the Church of Scotland, William ('Cardinal') Carstares, was desperately anxious to make Presbyterianism moderate and acceptable, and as Moderator of the General Assembly and Principal of Edinburgh University he strove mightily to that end. There was still widespread resentment, especially benorth the Forth, where Episcopalian ministers hung on with the support of the landowners, or when ousted entered noble households as chaplains, masters of music, tutors or even architects. Their committed Jacobite preaching ensured that the great bulk of active Scottish Jacobites always came from their flocks. The other religious group which tended to Jacobitism was the Roman Catholic community, but it was small, and apart from a pocket on the Borders, confined to relatively isolated regions in the North-East and the western part of the Highlands. There were, of course, always individual exceptions. There were Presbyterian Jacobites, and the head of the Roman Catholic church in the Highlands at the time of the '45 was privately deeply opposed to the whole business. Nevertheless, religious factors gave Jacobitism a stiffening of support in every rebellion.

The Williamite administration rapidly began to give offence even to firm supporters of the Revolution. William was a Stuart. He had come as much to preserve British government from the consequences of James VII and II, as he had to save the British from their king. In Scotland tarnished figures in the exiled monarch's service, such as Sir James Dalrymple and his son Sir John, were retained by William on the ground of their staunch defence of the royal prerogative. Only a strong prerogative could have kept them in office. William grudgingly accepted the abolition of the steering committee known as the Lords of the Articles which the Stuarts had always used as a device to emasculate the Scots parliament. However, throughout his reign he exerted every effort of influence and patronage at his disposal to minimise the implications of this new freedom for the legislature. William was obsessed with his great war against France. It raged from 1688 to 1697, with disastrous consequences for the Scots, whose overseas trade suffered dreadfully. To William Scotland was just a source of soldiers and taxes to help him play the Great European Game. Though he could not do anything about it, the terrible famine of the 1690s increased the unpopularity of his regime. Jacobite pulpits rang to the theme that here was a judgement of God against an erring nation.

Government ineptitude did not help. Confiscation of the estates of declared rebels was a standard political move, but it was not facilitated by Scots law, which carefully restricted the penalties for treason, nor much encouraged by Scots lawyers, who as landowners themselves disliked confiscation of land on principle. William's attempt to confiscate Dundee's estates became a notorious legal mess, and there was worse to follow. The Setons of Fyvie Castle (between Aberdeen and Banff) were the sort of hereditary Stuart civil servants likely to be Jacobite. After Killiecrankie the head of the family, Lord Dunfermline, fled to France with King James. In 1695 with an incompetence bordering on genius King William tried to give the estate not to one but to two supporters, Sir Thomas Livingston and James fourth Earl of Linlithgow. The resulting dispute ensured that the government only rid itself of the Fyvie property in 1733 by sale to William second Earl of Aberdeen. Scottish politics in the reign of William have been denounced as a turmoil due to the selfish feuding of magnate politicians. No doubt they were every bit as selfish and bloody-minded as their counterparts at Westminster, but much of the turmoil is explained by the assumption that the Scots in 1688 found they had exchanged one high-handed and unsympathetic government for another.

Much of the resulting resentment was focused by a particularly appalling episode in the Highlands. Under the Cromwellian regime the Highlands had been ruled effectively by a mixture of firmness and conciliation. To daunt the western clans, a fort had been built at Inverlochy in Lochaber in 1654. Situated at the head of a sea loch,

*3. Craigievar Castle, a classic example of the Scottish tower house,
now in the care of the National Trust for Scotland*

4. *Craigievar, the Great Hall*

*Fyvie Castle, the forfeited seat of the Jacobite Setons of Fyvie,
recently transferred to the care of the National Trust
for Scotland*

Loch Linnhe, and at the mouth of the Great Glen, which runs up to
Inverness, it was a strategic point which could be supplied by the
navy. As the brief civil war of the Revolution sputtered out in defeat,
negotiation, and bribery, it was an obvious ploy for the government
to reactivate Inverlochy, rechristened Fort William. To command it,
the veteran Colonel John Hill was recalled from Ireland as Governor. He had previously held the post under Cromwell.

The new government of Scotland was reluctant to commit sufficient resources to establish a firm grip on the Highlands. The civil
war was ending with an absurd palaver in which a group of West
Highland Chiefs headed by Lochiel condescended to make peace
with the Scottish government, after a significant distribution of
bribes on behalf of that government by the second greatest Campbell chief, the Earl of Breadalbane, and even then only after the Jacobite chiefs had ostentatiously taken time to ask the permission of the
exiled King James to desist from their efforts on his behalf. Given the
very high degree of acquiescence and active cooperation which the
Commonwealth regime had commanded from old Lochiel, this was
nonsense. Colonel Hill warned against any attempt to recruit troops

locally, on the grounds of their political unreliability, but that simply underlined the need for adequate regular forces. To commit substantial bodies of troops in Scotland was, however, the last thing King William wanted to do. The way to his favour was to suggest how they might safely be withdrawn to Flanders. Secretary of State Sir John Dalrymple, Master of Stair, a hater of Jacobites and a despiser of Highlanders, was sure that he had the answer.

He spent most of his working time either in his apartments in Kensington Palace or in William's field headquarters in Flanders. Of the 1,500 horse and 5,000 foot in Scotland, Stair singled out one infantry regiment as peculiarly suitable for his purposes. This was Argyll's regiment, officered by Campbell gentry, amongst them Robert Campbell of Glenlyon, a Campbell laird whose lands had been so ravaged by MacDonell of Keppoch and the MacDonalds of Glencoe in 1689, that he had been forced into the army at the advanced age of 59 to try to repair his fortunes. The idea that a 'Campbell' regiment such as this one was composed of a solid block of 8-900 Campbells is belied by the regimental list, which shows comparatively few rankers of that name. Over time people tended to adopt the name of the preponderant local magnate, but in the late seventeenth century the process was very incomplete. For example, many groups who called themselves Mackenzie in the eighteenth century, had in the sixteenth been known as Macraes, Murchisons, Maclays, Maclennans, Mathewsons, Macaulays, Morrisons, or MacLeods. In 1746 thirty families in the Braes of Lochaber by the name of McGlasserich, who normally lived surrounded by very Jacobite MacDonalds and who had been coerced into joining the Jacobite rebellion in 1745, changed their name to Campbell to indicate both their Whig identity, and their liberation from the MacDonalds of Keppoch.

In 1691 the Master of Stair was looking for a small Jacobite community which could be said to be defying the Williamite government. It might then be possible to inflict upon it the most draconian form of what was known as 'military execution' which was basically a mixture of plunder, rape and massacre. In theory one such act of frightfulness might effectively terrorise the much larger ascendancies, such as that of the Camerons of Lochiel, known to have Jacobite sympathies. The MacDonalds of Glencoe, the Clan Iain Abrach, whose chief was the MacIain, had the misfortune to fit the Master's list of requirements rather well. They were a small community living in a very well-defined locality. From the east Glencoe is almost unbelievably forbidding. On the north the glen is bordered by the unbroken ridge of the Aonach Eagach, with its 3,000-foot cliff faces. To the south soar some of the great peaks of the western Highlands, notably Buachaille Etive Mor and Buchaille Etive Beag, the Great and the Little Herdsmen of Etive. Their rock faces are so severe that they rank among the classic rock-climbing areas of modern Scotland. Further along, where the glen twists north-west towards Loch Leven, the setting is gentler. There are meadows around Loch Achtriochtan, and place names such as Achnacon ('the field of the dogs'). The bulk of the MacIain's people lived here in a series of clachans scattered from Achtriochtan to Invercoe. They lived, in other words, in something like a natural trap.

They were far from popular amongst their neighbours, because of their unsavoury reputation as cattle thieves. The precise nature of their religious allegiance has remained a matter for dispute to this day, but whatever it was, it was not such as to endear them to the new Presbyterian Establishment. Like Keppoch's people, they had exploited the turmoil of 1688-9 to predate on richer areas. They were by no means the most blatantly Jacobite of the west Highland clans. That distinction probably belonged to the MacDonalds of Glengarry whose chief, safe in the remoteness of his wooded strongholds to the west of the Great Glen, was indulging in flamboyant gestures such as entertaining the defeated General Cannon, and writing to Edinburgh as if he were an independent power. No government which meant to survive could possibly tolerate this. It was inevitable that King William would set a deadline by which all Highland chiefs had to recognise his authority on pain of a renewed offensive, not only by land forces, but also by naval units which were being moved into the waters of the Inner Hebrides. The deadline was the first of January 1692. The Jacobite chiefs waited for news from King James that he had no objections to them taking the oath. It was dangerous bravado, for news from the exiled monarch came through only late in December. Colonel Hill's own regiment had been driven to the verge of mutiny by government penny-pinching, but Argyll's regiment was ordered north from Inveraray, and the cautious Hill had been given as second-in-command the ruthless Lieutenant Colonel James Hamilton, a correspondent of the Master of Stair.

Alasdair MacDonald of Glencoe, the elderly chief of the Clan Iain Abrach more or less selected himself as the sacrificial lamb. At the very end of December he turned up at Fort William to ask Governor Hill to administer the oath which would entitle him to King William's indemnity. It was a fatal mistake. Hill had no power to administer the oath. For that the status of a royal sheriff was required, and the nearest man with such authority was Sir Colin Campbell of Ardkinglas, believed to be at Inveraray. After a desperate journey through snow the MacIain reached Inveraray on January 2nd, to find Sir Colin out of town celebrating Hogmanay with relatives. When he returned on January 5th, Sir Colin was quite understandably furious with the MacDonald chief. Most of the other Jacobite chiefs had met the deadline. They had all known about it for five solid months. To be late was inexcusable impudence richly meriting retaliation. If the Glencoe MacDonalds wanted war, they could have it. At that prospect, the MacIain wept, as well he might, and Sir Colin administered the oath. Ardkinglas was a humane and honourable gentleman, but even he had to warn the Glencoe chief that by any standards the Clan Iain Abrach was pressing its luck to breaking point.

Ardkinglas's certificate of 6 January, admitting the MacIain to King William's peace was technically invalid and was therefore cancelled. However, even those who had been advocating strong action against the recalcitrant Jacobite clans towards the end of 1691 were appalled at what followed. The Master of Stair had had his eye upon the Glencoe people from the end of that year. By early January 1692 he was writing to the Commander-in-Chief Scotland, Sir Thomas Livingstone, urging him to strike ruthlessly at oath-refusing rebels, and not to trouble with prisoners. Further orders of 11 January, and final orders signed and countersigned by King William and sent on 16 January, left no doubt that the Glencoe people were to be wiped out. By the end of the month Governor Hill was being advised 'let it be secret and suddain'. It was both, and it was also botched.

Campbell of Glenlyon was sent to Glencoe with a significant proportion of Argyll's regiment. He received orders to perpetrate a massacre on 12 February, after he and his men had been living as guests in the clachans for some days. On 13 February, he tried to carry out his instructions, but snow and bitter weather prevented Lieutenant-Colonel Hamilton from sealing off the glen with additional forces, and two of the chief's sons were prompt in leading the bulk of the clan to safety through the hills, at the cost of several deaths from exposure. Cunning and unscrupulous men like Breadalbane were appalled when they heard of the episode. He argued that the massacre would be counter-productive. A small clan had clearly been picked out because it was more vulnerable than say the MacLeans of Duart or the MacDonalds of Glengarry. This was not the first massacre in Highland history, and the death of the old chief and

A bleak winter at the entrance to Glencoe, scene of the massacre in 1692, now cared for by the National Trust for Scotland

37 others hardly rates more than a passing mention by the standards of the appalling twentieth century. Cromwellian troops had massacred far more people in both Dundee and Kirkcaldy during the latter stages of the mid seventeenth-century civil wars.

However, all of this misses the point. The massacre of 1692 went off at half cock, and totally failed to intimidate even the MacDonalds of Glencoe, who stood to arms and sent out war patrols as soon as they had settled in temporary homes in neighbouring glens. Lochiel and his Camerons also stood to arms, contemptuously ejecting any government forces billeted on them. Whigs who objected violently to the autocratic style of Charles II or James VII in Scotland could scarcely defend the Massacre of Glencoe. Whigs who genuinely wanted a new style of government after 1688 were deeply distressed, not only by the atrocity, but also by the way in which the government covered up for its perpetrators by a mixture of bureaucratic obstruction and systematic whitewash. Parliamentary pressure in the period 1693-95 did compel Sir James Dalrymple, Master of Stair, to retire from office, but William defied the Scots parliament's attempts to organise a serious investigation or prosecution. The whole mess was a propaganda gift of a high order to the exiled Stuarts, and was relentlessly exploited, first by the French and then by the English and Scots Jacobites.

William's government moved from crisis to crisis. By 1695 the Scottish economy was deteriorating, and William acceded to a plan to charter a new trade initiative in the shape of the Company of Scotland Trading to Africa and the Indies. It was to have a monopoly of Scottish trade with America, Africa and Asia. The English East India Company, originally chartered by Queen Elizabeth on the last day of 1600, rightly saw massive participation by English capital in this new venture as merely a device to suborn its own monopoly of English trade with the Orient. Because of its excessive identification with the late Stuart regime, the English East India Company had been fighting for its life since the Revolution. It did manage to block any English subscription to the Scots rival, sending Scottish national sentiment into a paroxysm of rage which made it lethally gullible when the plausible London Scot, William Paterson, suggested that the resources of the Company of Scotland be devoted to the creation of a trading colony on the isthmus of Darien in Central America. This gate of the world poised between the Pacific and the Caribbean was in fact unhealthy rain forest claimed by Spain, the last country William wanted to provoke because of the delicacy of the question of the succession to the Spanish realms after the death of the ailing Charles II of Spain who died in November 1700. The Scots would have lost everything in this venture anyway, but the refusal of England to help added fuel to the fire of resentment. The propertied classes of Scotland, including not a few Whig Highlanders, lost a fortune. Jacobite propagandists like Dr Archibald Pitcairne crowed with glee.

After the final Darien débâcle in 1700, the Scottish scene was envenomed. William died in 1702 urging the abolition of the Scots parliament by union with England, presumably on the grounds that if the temperature is intolerable, people will be less resentful if the thermometer is removed. Queen Anne was at first much less militant on the subject of Anglo-Scottish parliamentary union, but there was one absolutely basic issue which she knew had to be solved in her reign. This was the question of the succession. The death of her own last surviving child in July 1700 had provoked the English parliament into passing in 1701 an Act of Settlement which transferred the succession to the Electress of Hanover and her heirs. The Scots were not consulted. Their own radical Whigs, led by the uncompromising patriot laird, Andrew Fletcher of Saltoun, were anxious to use the succession question to compel a renegotiation of the terms of association with England, which virtually all Scots were convinced was strangling the development of the smaller country. Fletcher pointed out with justice that Scotland was being dragged into England's wars, and being heavily taxed to pay for them, whilst being systematically excluded by the Acts of Navigation from access to English and colonial markets. Most Scots seem to have hoped to use the succession crisis as a lever to compel the English to withdraw trade discrimination. The weakness in this policy was that, as Fletcher pointed out, the leading English politicians already controlled the Scottish executive, by reason of their grip on Crown patronage.

The exiled court of the Stuarts, based at the vast and rather gloomy palace of St Germains, not too far from Paris, contemplated the stormy politics of Scotland with rising hope. Louis XIV may not have been prepared to give them a fleet and an army, but his emotional commitment to their cause was beyond question. At the height of the great and cripplingly costly War of the Spanish Succession, which began in 1702, he was spending more on the exiled court than on the roads and bridges of France. The trouble was that their agents in the British Isles tended either to cock-eyed over-optimism or devious skullduggery. An interesting example of the latter was Simon Fraser of Beaufort, self-titled Lord Lovat. He was not technically the chief of Clan Fraser — the head of the name of Fraser was Lord Saltoun. Simon was the rightful heir to the Fraser of Lovat estates around Inverness. Ousted by the machinations of the Earl of Seaforth and his Mackenzies, Simon had tried to hit back by a gambit which involved the abduction and rape of a daughter of the House of Atholl. Scotland being too hot to hold him, he turned up at St Germains, whence he came back to Britain in 1703, ostensibly to spy out the land for a Jacobite rising. In practice he turned double agent, hoping to destroy Atholl and ingratiate himself with the Westminster government by smearing their leading 'country' opponents in the Scots parliament as crypto-Jacobites. Forewarned, Atholl successfully repudiated Simon's heroic implausibilities and left Westminster's principal man of business in Scotland, the Duke of Queensberry, discredited.

By 1704 the leading English politicians were becoming desperately worried about the Scottish situation. They were in the middle of a great war with France. A conciliatory Scottish ministry had been set up under Lord Tweeddale, but even it had failed to settle the

Scottish succession along the lines of the English one. To secure any taxes in Scotland, the Crown was being compelled to accede to legislation which made future Scottish participation in English wars very uncertain. Incorporating parliamentary union suddenly became in 1704 the central pillar of England's Scottish policy. John Dalrymple, First Earl of Stair, emerged from the mists of the Glencoe Massacre to be its passionate advocate, joining other voices such as the writer Daniel Defoe (sent up by London as a spy and propagandist) and the uncrushable William Paterson. Against them were ranged 'country' (i.e. anti-government) Whigs such as Andrew Fletcher of Saltoun and Lord Belhaven. Their objections were perhaps more to the manner of unification than to a closer association as such. What has worn best in their arguments is their deep distrust of a potentially irresponsible British executive which was determined to pull down any structures which would compel it to hold a dialogue with regional assemblies. Already an Alien Act passed by the Westminster legislature threatened the Scots with all-out economic warfare if by Christmas 1705 they were not on the way to incorporating union. Like many 'Great Debates' the one on the terms of the union was futile. The issue was settled by pressure on the Scots aristocracy coupled with a pre-arranged package of terms, conciliatory of propertied vested interests. For the Westminster government two Scots, the Duke of Queensberry and the Earl of Mar acted as managers. Their master-stroke was to buy the acquiescence of the disreputable and debt-ridden second Duke of Hamilton, nominal leader of the 'country' opposition. By 1707 the Act of Union was a fact. Scotland was abolished, in law.

From a Jacobite point of view, this was a political gift. The Presbyterian Whig patriot tradition was now obviously bankrupt. The Act of Union was clearly desperately unpopular. Its opponents said so. Its champions, such as Argyll, noisily denied this, but their actions belied their words. They too thought it deeply unpopular. After all, they laid down the procedure for the selection of the first Scottish MPs and peers at Westminster, and they simply refused to have real elections, for fear of the consequences. These 45 MPs and 16 'representative' peers, whose venality was rapidly to become and remain notorious, were selected by the discredited and doomed Scots parliament. Only Jacobites would use force to break the Union.

In St Germains, the new Jacobite claimant James Francis Edward Stuart felt that his time had come. From 1703 to 1707 one of his agents, Colonel Nathaniel Hooke, had been acting as a liaison between the French government and the Scottish Jacobites. Hooke had also spent a good deal of time with that slippery but ingenious rogue Simon Fraser of Beaufort who was hanging around the exiled court. Between them Hooke and Fraser hatched a plan which made a great deal of strategic sense, not just from a Jacobite but also from a purely French point of view. In 1707, immediately after the passage of the Act of Union, Hooke returned to Paris with a memorandum from many influential Scots to Louis XIV, in which the signatories asked for French backing for an expedition by James, promising that 'the moment their King lands, the whole nation will rise and dissolve the present Government'. Hooke's argument was that if James could seize control of Scotland, and then imitate the behaviour of seventeenth-century Scottish opponents of his own grandfather Charles I, by occupying the Tyne-Tees coalfields in north-east England, the London government would be forced to negotiate for an end to the current war with France. London's coal supply came entirely from the Tyne-Tees area.

It was a not unreasonable plan. France wanted out of a crippling and unsuccessful war with England. By March 1708 Louis had organised a small flotilla of five warships and several swift privateers at Dunkirk, to carry the 19-year-old Pretender and a body of French troops to Scotland. James carried proclamations addressed only to his Scottish subjects. As far as we can see, this expedition was designed with the moderate aim of restoring him to one realm, and at the same time of forcing England to the negotiating table. Bad luck and bad management combined to wreck a good opportunity. With his usual miserable luck, James caught measles at Dunkirk, and delayed everything. When he recovered, the expedition did set sail, but it rapidly became clear that the naval commander, Admiral Count Claude de Forbin, had absolutely no faith in his own mission. He would have preferred not to sail, and was full of glee when the voyage turned out to be so stormy that James and his followers were very seasick. The military commander, the Count de Gace, was equally negative, seeing himself and his officers as a doomed forlorn hope. Casting anchor in the mouth of the Firth of Forth opposite the East Neuk of Fife, the Jacobites prepared to land at Burntisland and advance to seize Stirling. Jacobite lairds were already in arms to greet them. The British general officer in command in Scotland subsequently said that the forces in Scotland were so scandalously weak that he could not have resisted any landing or rising, and indeed would have had to retire on Berwick. At this point Admiral Byng appeared with a Royal Navy squadron. Forbin fled north despite the tears and pleas of James to be put ashore in Fife, at Montrose, or on the Aberdeenshire coast. With the loss of one vessel, Forbin escaped round the British Isles to return to France with an even sicker James. The London government had had a very lucky escape.

A medallion showing the Whig view of the '08, French ships fleeing and Jacobite prisoners being led to the Tower of London

CHAPTER IV

'The Great Rising — the '15'

OF ALL THE JACOBITE RISINGS, THERE IS NO DOUBT that it is the '45 which has lingered longest in popular memory. Yet the 1715 was a far bigger rising, and it had a far better chance of success at the outset, not least because the Scottish rising was aided by the outbreak of a small Jacobite rebellion in the north-east of England. Another paradoxical feature of the 1715 was the fact that it drew only the slenderest of support from the international connections of Jacobitism. It would be quite wrong to suggest that the history of Jacobitism can be written exclusively from a Scottish point of view. English Jacobitism was real and widespread in certain circles, if elusive when the call came to substitute Jacobite deeds for Jacobite words, but above all Jacobitism had an international dimension from the moment King James took the field with French troops in his army in Ireland after he had fled from England. The exiled Stuarts assumed rightly that there was considerable sympathy for their plight in Roman Catholic Europe. The Hanoverians who succeeded to the British and Irish thrones in 1714 were seen as Protestant usurpers. In France, Spain, Austria, and the Italian principalities, there was widespread emotional support for the exiled house. King James VII and II, haunted by sexual guilt feelings assiduously encouraged by his wife, turned more and more to prayer and mortification in his latter years, and there were perfectly serious proposals to start a process for his beatification after his death.

The exiled dynasty frequently sought support from non-Catholic powers such as Sweden or Russia. In conversation with Protestants their representatives always insisted that the Jacobite cause had absolutely nothing to do with religion. Obviously, it was largely a question of circumstance and audience how the Jacobite case was presented, but one point was always pretty clear. The only European power with the basic strength to intervene so massively in the

British Isles as to compel the complete or partial restoration of the Stuarts was France. Only if the exiled line became the first priority of French strategists was its restoration a highly probable event. There lay the rub, for France was always faced with more demands on its strength than it could possibly meet in full. King Louis XIV, with his deep commitment to hereditary right and royal absolutism, still had to think primarily about winning when France was at war. He did indeed send his heralds to St Germains, when he heard of the death of James VII and II in 1701, to have the late exile's son proclaimed 'James VIII and III' of Scotland, England and Ireland. Yet he hastened to assure the London government that all of this was purely nominal, and towards the latter stages of the War of the Spanish Succession, Louis XIV was struggling desperately to avoid defeat and humiliation.

By the Peace of Utrecht of 1713, Louis was compelled not only to recognise the Protestant Succession in Britain, but also to expel the Jacobite court from his realm. James Francis Edward Stuart moved himself and his entourage to Bar-le-Duc in the then independent Duchy of Lorraine. Of course, the pledged public word of Louis XIV, the Most Christian King of France, was notoriously worthless if his public pledges ran contrary to his private prejudices. He had no intention of totally withdrawing his sponsorship from the man he had recognised as legitimate heir to James VII and II. To avoid public provocation, he wrote to his grandson Philip V of Spain asking him to fund the Jacobites, secretly. A treaty was signed between Philip V and James. It offered money in exchange for two undertakings from James in the event of his restoration. The first was that Britain would support certain Spanish territorial claims in Italy. The second undertaking was the restoration of the Roman Catholic religion, first in Ireland and then in the rest of the British Isles. Despite the high-flown language of the secret treaty, Spain had no serious intention of handing over money until there were signs that the Jacobites were near to seizing power. At that point Spain was likely to activate the treaty, in order to establish a claim on the gratitude of the new British government. In September 1714 Louis XIV died, and the prospects for James grew bleak indeed.

George I had been proclaimed and had succeeded to the British thrones without the least difficulty. Queen Anne did not like him personally, but she always intended that her Hanoverian relatives should succeed her. Of the two great political parties whose rivalries so disturbed her realms, the Whigs were totally committed to the Protestant Succession, while the Tories under their quarrelling leaders Harley and Bolingbroke actually presided over the accession of George I. Even Bolingbroke knew perfectly well that James was not a viable candidate unless he was prepared to change his religion. This James would not do. Worse still, from the point of view of Jacobite political hopes, was the fact that the new ruler of France on behalf of the five-year-old Louis XV was Philip Duke of Orleans, nephew of the late monarch. Orleans, like everyone else, thought that in an age of high child mortality Louis XV would probably not reach his majority. Most Frenchmen regarded Charles V of Spain as the next legitimate claimant, so Charles had no intentions of respecting his own waiver of such a claim in the Treaty of Utrecht. Orleans therefore needed peace and indeed an understanding with Britain in order to secure his own position. The Hanoverian and Orleanist successions were linked.

The Jacobite cause in Britain, and more particularly in Scotland, had actually never been healthier. The particular resentments of patriotic Scots were likely to be far more dangerous to a Westminster government if they could ally with widespread discontent in English society. That discontent the new Hanoverian dynasty and its close Whig allies soon set about providing. The party divisions of Anne's reign, Whig and Tory, proved durable, though they were complicated by the fact that when the Whigs moved, as they did in 1715-16, into an almost exclusive monopoly of office, they themselves split into a Court Whig party, entrenched in office, and a Country Whig faction of excluded Whigs who devoted much of their time to the search for issues on which they could form a tactical alliance with the Tories. They had to expend energy on their search because the idelogical barriers between them and the Tories were so high. At the start of the new regime it was an obvious Whig tactic to try to identify Toryism with Jacobitism, and one way of doing this was to threaten the lives of Tory leaders like Harley and Bolingbroke, in the hope that they would cut and run for the only alternative court — the Jacobite one. Harley sat out the campaign against him. Bolingbroke's nerve snapped under the threat of impeachment for high treason. He fled to James, whose first minister he rapidly became. The great Tory political and military hero, the Duke of Ormonde, was likewise persuaded to retire to the Continent, where he rapidly emerged as the liaison between James and Spain.

In general, Tories found themselves systematically excluded from positions of profit and power. Their strong attachment to the concept of hereditary right had been much reassured by the presence of the English throne of an undoubted royal Stuart in the rather baggy shape of Queen Anne. Now, with a Hanoverian apparently sustaining a Court Whig monopoly of power (which in fact was too absolute for the personal preferences of either George I or George II, but which they found difficult to avoid), the Tories' ambiguous relationship with Jacobitism became a much more serious matter.

An extreme example of this was the leading Scots politician, the Earl of Mar, known as 'Bobbing John' because of his lack of consistency. He had been an architect of the Act of Union of 1707 and despite his association with Anne's last government, which was not exactly a recommendation in the eyes of George I, he hoped to survive in office under the Hanoverians. He had estates in the Lowlands near Alloa, and in the Highlands on Deeside, but he needed his official salary and his ego had become used to the consolations of ministerial rank. In his own memoirs Mar stated that he had been in correspondence with St Germains for four years before the death of Queen Anne. The radical possibility exists that he was telling the truth, but if so this correspondence was strictly fire insurance, for nobody excelled Mar in grovelling sycophancy towards George I. He even got up an absurd address to the new monarch, designed to be signed by Highland chiefs as a demonstration to their enthusiastic loyalty. Mar had an agent wandering round the Highlands touting this document, which was couched in the most extravagant terms, and he secured quite a few signatures. Most of the signatories joined Mar in active rebellion shortly afterwards. George I made the mistake of turning his back on Mar at a reception. Knowing that there would be no job for him, the disgruntled politician boarded one of the vast fleet of colliers continually sailing up the east coast of England to the Tyneside coal-field whence London drew its fuel. From there he progressed to Fife, and from Fife to Deeside where he summoned chiefs and nobles to a conspiracy thinly disguised as a hunting party. Early in September 1715 Mar raised the Jacobite standard on the Braes of Mar.

Clearly, personal charisma on the part of Mar hardly explains the enthusiastic response he received. He had to make repeal of the much-disliked Act of Union a central commitment of his movement. Since he had helped pass it in the first place, he had to do a lot of fast talking from the start. Mar was a light to a powder keg of discontent. It hardly mattered that as Jacobite lights went he was rather a dim one. The Scottish nobility and gentry, with representatives of whom he was closeted for several anxious days before he raised the standard, had simply had enough.

Conservative intellectuals like Dr Archibald Pitcairne, the Edinburgh physician, Jacobite, wag, and wit, had sustained a steady stream of propaganda denouncing the Revolution of 1688 as the opening of the floodgates to social and political radicalism allied to vulgar religious fanaticism. The argument was clearly vastly exaggerated, but it reflected deep-felt conflicts within Scottish society. Apart from the clash between presbyterian and episcopal concepts of government for the Kirk by Law Established, there was the whole question of the future development of Scottish culture. Pitcairne was a poet in the Latin language. Because Scots was a minority language, difficult for even an English person to follow in its late medieval or early modern written form, Scottish writers had always tended to use Latin when they wanted access to a European audience. In the sixteenth century the most distinguished Scottish Latinist was the great humanist George Buchanan. His political views were sufficiently radical for his best-known writings to be burned as dangerous by the loyal and learned University of Oxford after the Restoration of the Stuarts in 1660. By the seventeenth century it was the royalist Arthur Johnston who was the prince of Scottish Latin poets, and by Pitcairne's time the defenders of Scotland's Latin heritage tended to be Jacobites. Thomas Ruddiman, an outstanding eighteenth-century Scottish Latinist and publisher, was one.

These conservative intellectuals, who included clergy of an Episcopal persuasion, were not without influence. Ruddiman was for many years Assistant Librarian and later Librarian to the Society of Advocates, the influential body of Edinburgh lawyers who dominated the Scottish legal profession. Pitcairne was well-known in the leading social circles of the Scottish capital. In 1731 his daughter Janet was to become the second wife of the fifth Earl of Kellie, whose family name was Erskine. They had risen to the peerage through the patronage of James VI and I in the early seventeenth century, so they were likely to be instinctive supporters of the main Stuart line. The fifth Earl of Kellie was in fact a Jacobite colonel who fought in both the '15 and '45. His eldest son, Alexander Thomas Erskine, sixth Earl of Kellie, had to cope with the collapse of Jacobite politics, and with the sad fact that the stigma of past Jacobite sympathies was likely to blight his chances of promotion in any normal career, as it blighted the military careers of his brothers. The sixth Earl of Kellie in fact coped very well by becoming the best-known native British musical composer of his day. Had the dice of war rolled differently in 1715 or 1745 Pitcairne's grandson might have been the dominant political magnate in Fife, instead of selling the estates to a Whig politician in order to concentrate on music.

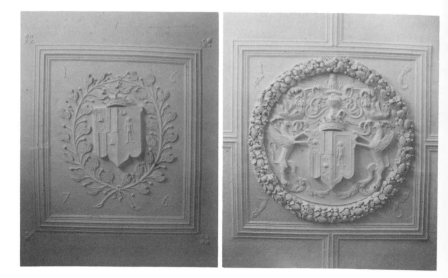

The central panels of two of the ceilings in Kellie Castle show
the Arms of Erskine and Dalzell,
families with strong Jacobite connections

Whereas no great peer had rallied to Dundee's standard, there was a good deal of magnate support for Mar. The dashing young fifth Earl of Southesk, for example, the hero of the song 'the Piper of Dundee', met with Mar at Aboyne on Deeside and returned home to Angus to raise a cavalry force for the Jacobite army. His older friend James Maule, fourth Earl of Panmure, took a small boat north from Edinburgh in order to join the rebellion. He proclaimed 'James VIII and III' in the town of Brechin where he had a great deal of influence. The fact that a cautious man of his age was prepared to rebel was thought by at least one Hanoverian observer to show that the Jacobites thought the game was as good as won. James Lord Ogilvy, heir to the Earl of Airlie, and the young Earl of Strathmore, expressed the strong hostility of their families to the Act of Union by coming out in rebellion. Needless to say, the great families of the North-East were well to the fore in the Jacobite cause. George Keith, tenth and last Earl Marischal of Scotland joined Mar with his significantly named younger brother James Francis Edward Keith. Together they proclaimed James VIII at the market cross in Aberdeen. Their principal seat was in fact Inverugie Castle near Peterhead, a town of which they were the feudal superiors and whose Jacobitism was thus so

5. *Kellie Castle, now in the care of the National Trust for Scotland, seat of a Jacobite family who found consolation in music after the '45*

6. *Killiecrankie, where Mackay's army was routed by Dundee.*
The battle site is now owned by the National Trust for Scotland

secure that the Chevalier made it his landfall in Scotland when he came to join his supporters.

In the Highlands there was very widespread support for the '15. Of the three great imperialist clans of the seventeenth century – the Mackenzies, the Gordons, and the Campbells one was strongly Jacobite, one half-heartedly so, and one the mainstay of the Whig cause in Scotland. The Duke of Argyll, the chief of Clan Campbell, was the Hanoverian commander in Scotland during the crisis of the rebellion. The Earl of Seaforth, chief of the Mackenzies, came out for 'James VIII', as did, in an unenthusiastic way, Alexander Marquis of Huntly, the heir to the Gordon chief, the dying first Duke of Gordon. Huntly had the difficult job of living between a passionately Jacobite mother, sister to Lord Strathmore, and an English Whig wife, Lady Henrietta Mordaunt, daughter of the eccentric Whig military hero, the Earl of Peterborough. Huntly joined Mar but conducted himself with such prudence, and abandoned the Jacobite cause so early, that he was allowed to succeed peacefully as second Duke of Gordon in 1716.

In other magnate houses the impact of the '15 was much more traumatic. John, second Marquess and first Duke of Atholl, had been a supporter of the Revolution and was a devoted subject of Queen Anne whom he said in 1704 he would fight for 'not only against Papists, but also against either Whig or Tory, if they prove her enemies.' He was a distruster of Westminster politicians and an opponent of the Act of Union, but sufficiently sound in the Hanoverian interest to be made Lord Lieutenant of Perthshire in 1715. He was already the royal sheriff of Perthshire for life, and this gave him control over that smaller part of the county which did not come within the jurisdiction of his vast hereditary Regality of Atholl where he presided with literally kingly powers. His eldest son John had been killed fighting in Flanders in the British army commanded by the Duke of Marlborough at the Battle of Malplaquet in 1709. His second son William, called Marquess of Tullibardine after his elder brother's death, had been a student at the notoriously Jacobite St Leonard's College in the University of St Andrews. He joined the rebellion under Mar along with his younger brothers Charles and George (the future Jacobite General of the '45). As a result, he was attainted of high treason by the Westminster Parliament in 1716. His father secured the family succession by obtaining another piece of legislation which transferred the succession to his third son, Lord James, who duly became the second or Hanoverian Duke of Atholl, as distinct from Duke William, the Jacobite Duke.

Despite their father's opposition the younger members of the Atholl family were able to raise an Atholl Brigade for the Jacobite Army. It took its place in a line of battle full of Highland troops. Clans such as the MacGregors, the Keppoch and Glengarry Mac-Donells, and the MacLeans were almost automatic participants in a Jacobite rising, even though the leading MacGregor of the day (though not the accepted clan chief, for there was none) Rob Roy, turned out to be a very cautious warrior indeed. His philosophy, 'if they cannot win without us, they certainly will not win with us', would if generally embraced have largely freed Mankind from the scourge of War. In an age of passionate allegiances, where religion was the context of most social and political life, Rob had a truly remarkable flair for detachment. His arch-enemy was the Duke of Montrose, a ScottishWhig belonging to the Squadrone faction, best known for its hostility to the other leading Scottish Whig faction, the Argathelians or followers of Argyll. Out of compliment to Argyll, Rob used the name Campbell for long periods, usually when only Argyll's influence stood between him and massive retribution for some of his less legal business ventures, such as the levying of black-mail. Rob also cultivated the patronage of the Roman Catholic and Jacobite House of Perth. Out of compliment to them, he adopted their religious views, but it must be said that his critical detachment towards the theology of the See of Rome was much the same as his qualified loyalty to the Clan Campbell.

Far more committed to the Jacobite cause was the Clan Cameron. Old Sir Ewen Cameron of Lochiel was too old to take the field, so his clansmen came out under his son John, who had incidentally been a signer of Mar's fulsome address to George I. For him there was to be no going back on his decision to come out in 1715. Support for the rising was so widespread that there were even Campbells in Mar's ranks, though of course they showed little zeal for attacks on their kinsmen in Argyll. These clansmen came from the central Highland ascendancy of Sir John Campbell, first Earl of Breadalbane, whose nickname, 'Grey John', was supplemented by the description 'cunning as a fox, wise as a serpent'. From his seat in Glenorchy this scheming Campbell rival of Argyll looked out over Scottish politics, seldom committing his person, but always aiming at backing winners, and reaching for the leadership of the greatest of the clans (at least since the abolition of the MacDonald Lordship of the Isles in 1493). Like Huntly, Breadalbane turned out to be rather good at jumping off the Jacobite bandwagon when it ceased to roll.

Argyll, who tried to rally the pro-Hanoverian forces in what, as a good Unionist, he was supposed to call North Britain, was quite emphatic that north of the Forth there were nine Jacobites for every Whig. Even men whose position depended on government support like the leading contender for the disputed Fraser of Lovat heritage, Fraser of Fraserdale, joined the Jacobites. There were, of course, Whig pockets in the Highlands. Around Inverness the Roses of Kilravock and the Forbes of Culloden family were Whig by conviction. They acquired in the course of the rising an unlikely ally in the shape of Simon Fraser of Beaufort, Fraserdale's rival for the title and estates of Lovat. Simon probably came back to support King James, but rapidly worked out that it would pay better to back King George.

It must be emphasised that the towns tended to be every bit as keenly Jacobite as the landward areas. The burghs had been particularly resentful of the imposition of an English-type Customs and Excise administration after the Act of Union. They were not used to it, nor did they find its very protective high-tariff system appropriate for their own traditional North Sea trades, or for the needs of the Scottish economy, which needed to exchange raw materials for cheap manufactured goods from abroad. Smuggling had rapidly become a well-regarded national industry and riots against Customs and Excise officers, not to mention sackings of the King's Warehouse to recover confiscated goods, became a regular feature of life in east-coast burghs whose leading merchants and magistrates tended to the Episcopal persuasion in religion and the Jacobite in their politics. The Jacobite-inclined Bailie John Steuart of Inverness, factor for the Earl of Moray in the Lordship of Petty, whose principal seat was Castle Stuart, some four miles from Inverness, recorded with no enthusiasm in June 1715 that 'There is a mighty seizure of about 25 tunns brandy and some wine made by our Custom house officers here this week'. Bailie Steuart was not only a town magistrate, as his title indicates, but also an active smuggler. The Jacobites normally had no difficulty in taking over major burghs. In Aberdeen they simply announced an election in which any burgess could vote and found themselves a wholly amenable town council presided over by Provost Patrick Bannerman. Montrose had since 1707 a record of Jacobite-inspired unrest second to none. The magistracy of Arbroath were most cooperative with Mar while the behaviour of the municipal government of Dundee during the rising may be deduced from the fact that every single member of it found it prudent to disappear at the end of the campaign. The odd burgh where there was any resistance, like Fraserburgh, usually turned out to be a burgh of barony with a Whig feudal superior — in this case Lord Saltoun.

[In a private Scottish collection]

Major James Fraser of Castle Leathers in 1723,
wearing tartan trews and a large sporran,
with the black cockade of Hanover in his bonnet

The advantages enjoyed by the Jacobites in 1715 were thus very great. The Westminster parliament's ill-advised decision to abolish the Scots Privy Council in 1708 had deprived the Hanoverian regime of any effective executive body capable of trying to get a grip on any sudden crisis in Scotland. The Scots nobility, the men who had pushed the Act of Union through, had been progressively alienated, partly by the failure of the Scots economy to make the sort of spectacular progress brashly guaranteed by such unreliable and dishonest English propagandists as Daniel Defoe, and partly by very specific issues such as the refusal of the Westminster House of Lords to admit Scots peers on the strength of their British titles. This last point was particularly galling to the magnates, who had to scrabble for a place amongst the sixteen so-called 'Representative Peers', notoriously a list nominated by the government and pushed through by patronage and influence at a heavily manipulated election by Scots peers in Edinburgh.

Because Episcopalian clergy in Scotland were excluded from the Kirk by Law Established, most of them formed a ready-made Jacobite clerical intelligentsia which could replace Presbyterian ministers. At the start of any Jacobite rebellion they could at a moment's notice occupy parish kirk pulpits and start to preach support for the rising to a countryside and burghs seething with violent discontent. Nationalist emotions, by courtesy of Westminster, could only find expression in Jacobite actions, and even the bulk of Hanoverian supporters in Scotland were dispirited by the actions of the British government since 1707. In his *History of the Union,* first published in 1709, Defoe had to admit that the imposition of England's draconian and barbaric treason laws on Scotland had been carried against the will of virtually all Scotland, including even her venal representatives at Westminster. Committed Presbyterians had been shaken by the virtual parallel establishment of Episcopal clergy in Scotland pushed through by the very Tory last parliament of Queen Anne, a body apparently blissfully unaware that in Scotland such people were almost invariably rabid Jacobites.

It required real talent for Mar to lose the game, but he proved equal to the challenge. It is true that Argyll quickly positioned himself at Stirling with such forces as he could scrape together. Stirling Castle was the strategic heart of Scotland because of the way the River Firth posed an almost insurmountable obstacle to the progress of a large army. The Forth is a short river which escapes from the southern Highlands to meander across a carse or flood plain ten miles wide by forty long, before it plunges into its own huge Firth by

Stirling Castle
(from an engraving in John Slezer's Theatrum Scotiae, *1693)*

way of mud flats and tidal saltings. Until the late eighteenth century it was surrounded by extensive mosses or bogs which reduced the viable route between north and south to a narrow corridor domi- nated by the mighty royal fortress of Stirling Castle, perched precip- itously on its volcanic crag. To the west the mountains bar large- scale movement as far as Loch Lomond while west of that loch lay another extremely narrow strategic corridor dominated by the royal rock fortress of Dumbarton which would have to be tackled by any Jacobite army even if it had already forced its way past the Campbell country to the north. Behind Argyll lay a staunchly Whig Glasgow and south-west, an Edinburgh with a long record of deference to the established government, not to mention the greatest royal rock fortress of them all at the head of its one great central street.

On the other hand, nobody was more aware than Argyll that he could be outflanked, and he could be overwhelmed by superior fron- tal assault. Mar first formed a camp at Perth, where he received mas- sive reinforcement from Highlands and Lowlands. He had no great difficulty in slipping troops into Fife and taking over that rather unusual county. The politics of early modern society were essentially the politics of consensus in a deferential society. Decision tended to be slow but virtually unanimous and led by the aristocracy. In Fife the lairds were often strongly Jacobite, but a mixture of religious radicalism and close trading links with the Protestant Netherlands ensured that many of the Fife trading burghs were incorrigibly Whig. They could not stop Mar from resting his left flank on the north shore of the Forth. Arms intended for Lord Sutherland, the Hanoverian leader in the northern Highlands, were captured by the Jacobites at Burntisland.

Mar then threw out two striking forces to the west and south. The soundness of his judgement in doing this may be gravely questioned. He wholly violated the military maxim of concentration of forces, unless he had ordered the commanders of these forces to fall on Argyll's flanks whilst he simultaneously launched a furious frontal offensive. Instead General Alexander Gordon of Auchintoul was sent off to wage war in Argyll and capture Inveraray as a prelude to marching on Dumbarton and Glasgow. The Campbell lairds saw to the defence of that small burgh on Loch Fyne, which was effectively the clan capital. They did so despite the presence of Argyll's brother the Earl of Ilay, a professional politician who turned out to be a pompous, useless fusspot in the midst of the realities of war. In any case the Jacobite assault, when it came, was unenthusiastic. The troops knew they were wasting time in the wrong place.

Worse still was Mar's misuse of his best soldier, Brigadier William Mackintosh of Borlum, who had captured Inverness at an early stage. The Mackenzies had no difficulty in dealing with Lord Sutherland and the northern Whig clans such as the Mackays and Munros. Borlum could therefore move south to Fife. On 12 October 1715 he crossed the Forth with 2,000 men in small fishing boats. Instead of swinging against Argyll's flank, he made a dash for Edinburgh, was repulsed, and wandered off south to join up with two other small Jacobite rebellions.

One was in the north-east of England where there was widespread discontent among a declining local gentry, often Roman Catholic or High Anglican and Tory. Excluded from offices of profit under the Crown, the Tories for political and the Catholics for religious reasons, they were suffering from declining incomes due to low agricultural prices, and a crisis in coal-mining due to drainage problems. Mining royalties were often a vital supplement to their rent rolls and the solution to the crisis of deep drainage, which

arrived too late to save many of them, came in the form of steam
engines first developed in the tin mines of Cornwall.

On 9 October a group of Jacobites proclaimed James at Wark-
worth and marched on Newcastle, which defied them. They were a
small group of gentry led by the young Earl of Derwentwater (a son
of one of the innumerable bastards of Charles II), his brother
Charles Radcliffe, Lord Widdrington, Charles and Nicholas Wogan,
and the local M.P. Mr Thomas Forster. Because he was one of the
few Protestants in this group of 'fox hunters armed with dress
swords', Forster had to be given command. He turned out as useless
a commander as Ilay or Mar. What he did do was link up with a tiny
Jacobite rising in the Scottish Borders, almost entirely explicable in
terms of the households of a handful of Roman Catholic aristocrats
led by Lords Kenmure, Nithsdale and Wintoun. The combined
group in turn linked up with Brigadier Mackintosh and eventually
marched south into Lancashire where it hoped to rouse the latent
Jacobitism of a large Roman Catholic population. They did route the
comic-opera force known as the posse-comitatus of Westmoreland,
but at Preston they were pinned down and brought to battle by the
combined forces of the Hanoverian Generals Carpenter and Wills.
The Jacobite army was outnumbered and trapped. Though it gave a
good account of itself in the first day of street fighting, its leaders lost
heart and surrendered.

Mar had meantime been waiting with a force superior to Argyll's,

A Hanoverian view of the '15: on one side of the medallion,
an aggressive George I; on the other, Jacobites fleeing
at Sheriffmuir from a symbolic figure of Avenging Justice

often by a margin of over one hundred per cent. When Argyll had four thousand men, Mar had ten thousand. The margin was so big that Mar did not need to defeat Argyll. All he had to do was fight, and Argyll could probably not have replaced a day's losses to allow a serious stand on the second day. Finally, far too late, Mar recalled General Gordon, and on 13 November, the same day on which Mackintosh and his men opened fire in the streets of Preston, the fate of the Jacobite rising was settled by the singularly indecisive battle of Sheriffmuir, fought above Dunblane. Both sides routed an enemy wing. Elsewhere the fighting was indecisive. Argyll expected to be overwhelmed by a fresh attack at dawn, but was amazed to find Mar had retreated. Early in the next month the Dutch honoured their commitment to the Protestant Succession in Britain by sending over 6,000 troops to defend it. Argyll kept telling Westminster that it did not grasp how lucky it had been. The southern Jacobite army had surrendered on 14 November. The military and psychological balance had swung decisively against the Jacobites before James Francis Edward Stuart landed at Peterhead, three days before Christmas in the bitter winter of 1715-16.

The poor man had been all eagerness to join his adherents. He probably had no serious control over Mar's decision to start the rebellion, nor had he any choice once his standard had been raised for him, except to endorse Mar's leadership; James was tired of being treated as a pawn by the French. He slipped through northern France in disguise before leaving Dunkirk in mid December in a small ship of 200 tons and eight guns. It was a hazardous journey because of the patrolling ships of the Royal Navy which were on the lookout for just such an attempt to run the rival candidate for the British thrones as if he were smuggled brandy (of which the ship carrying James also carried a cargo). As Peterhead proved the eventual landfall, it is hardly surprising that James caught a cold almost as soon as he landed on that exposed shoulder of the North-East. He moved to Fetteresso, the principal seat of the Earl Marischal, where he was duly proclaimed by Marischal and Mar. There he also received an effusively loyal address from the Episcopal clergy of the North-East, an address which of course was subsequently employed by their Presbyterian opponents as proof that they were unworthy of toleration by the Hanoverian regime. A guest of Lord Panmure at Brechin, of Lord Southesk at Kinnaird, and of the Strathmore family (whose young head died at Sheriffmuir) at Glamis, James duly reached Perth and set up a spartan court at Scone. He found his cause already lost. He undoubtedly had a better claim by Hereditary

Right than George I (who stood fifty-eighth in strict succession), but Providence was not working for him.

January saw a reinforced Argyll advance through thick snow on Perth. After burning several intervening villages in a vain attempt to hold up the Hanoverians, the Jacobites evacuated Perth on 30 January. James was deeply distressed by the burnings, but equally distressed by the collapse of his hopes. Late in December the exiled Jacobite court had been in receipt of significant sums of money from Spain. The Regent Orleans in France not only encouraged this subvention, but also toyed with the thought that the most profitable course for France might well be to back a successful Jacobite rising in Britain. Had Mar swept Argyll aside, linked up with the northern English Jacobites, and rallied the Roman Catholic population of Lancashire to his victorious standard, the new Hanoverian regime in England would certainly have had its back to the wall, and would probably have collapsed. Now even the Spaniards could see that the Jacobites were not succeeding. At last £15,000 of Spanish gold was despatched in a small ship from Calais in January, but the bad luck which dogged the whole rising ensured that it was wrecked on the sands of St Andrews Bay. The crew all escaped and Mar briefly hoped that he might recover the bullion, even though Hanoverian troops were pouring into Fife. It was not to be, for the month of February saw the Jacobite retreat continue up the east coast from Dundee to Montrose. On 3 February, James wrote a despairing plea to the Regent Orleans, saying that without French help his cause was lost. It was lost anyway, for the next day James shipped out of Montrose on a small ship the *Marie Thérèse* of St Malo, with Mar and Lord Drummond. They reached Gravelines a week later. Fittingly, Adam Cockburn, the Whig judge who was Lord Justice Clerk of Scotland, reported that the Spanish gold on the hulk on the West Sands at St Andrews was being fished up by the triumphant Hanoverian soldiery.

CHAPTER V

The
Little Rising —
the '19

WHEN JAMES AND MAR LEFT MONTROSE JACOBITISM was at a low ebb. It had failed to make anything of a range of opportunities which had stretched over a period of years and were unlikely to recur again on the same scale. It was not just a question of the military failures of late 1715 and early 1716, heartbreaking and decisive though these were. James had completely failed to take advantage of the dominance of a Tory regime in Britain from 1710 to 1714, despite the fact that the parliamentary Tory party contained a significant Jacobite wing. It was never a majority of the Tory party, most of whose MPs remained attached to the Protestant Succession and the Hanoverian interest, but a group of about fifty-seven Jacobite Tories should have given James significant leverage over the harassed and divided British government led by Harley and Bolingbroke.

The timing of the Tory triumph in 1710 was a good one from the point of view of the exiled Stuarts. They had tended to count on French support as the instrument which would restore them to their thrones. It had not been necessary to make any very serious concessions to their predominantly Protestant supporters in Britain, most of whom held militantly 'country' views, suspicious of what they saw as the arrogant and irresponsible authoritarianism of the 'court' politicians who dominated the executive. The exiled Stuarts very rapidly lost touch with the feelings of British Jacobites. James VII and II was not thought of in St Germains as a man who had made any mistakes in his style of government. There were in fact attempts to beatify him as late as 1734. In the inner core of the exiled court there was limited enthusiasm for Scottish opposition to the Act of Union. Before 1710 Protestants were conspicuously absent from the inner counsels of the Chevalier.

Then in 1710 the French position in the War of the Spanish Succession deteriorated to the point where there was no way in which troops and ships could be spared for an invasion of England on behalf of the Stuarts. James was thrown back on the loyalty of British Jacobites. Though there were always many Irish people at the Stuart court, James rightly assumed that his father's experience in Ireland in 1689-90 showed that the Irish kingdom was untentable without control over England. Jacobite strategy at the highest level therefore concentrated exclusively on England and Scotland, with Scotland after 1708 being seen as essentially a springboard for an attempt on England. Robert Harley, later Earl of Oxford, was well aware that the transition to a Hanoverian dynasty might be difficult and could be seriously impeded by astute manoeuvres by the Jacobites within his own party; they could manipulate the mounting rage of other Tory backbenchers at the persistent refusal of Harley's administration to implement a distinctively Tory policy. Harley therefore opened secret and bogus negotiations directly with the exiled court, whose members were increasingly out of touch with British realities, and by a series of bland expressions of good will persuaded James to order the Jacobite MPs and Peers to support Harley unconditionally. Reluctantly, the Jacobites in parliament obeyed their orders. It was a disastrous miscalculation by James. Harley had no intention of engineering a restoration. Even if James had announced his conversion (which nobody would have deemed sincere), Harley would have stayed with the House of Hanover. James had been fooled before he was defeated in battle.

At least he had not appeared as a mere stooge of a European power bent on causing mischief in Britain to serve its own ends. Within a year or two of the end of the '15 that additional humiliation was heaped on the unfortunate Jacobite cause. The roots of this particular disaster can be traced back to the treaty with Spain which had produced some inadequate and tardy financial backing from the Spanish court for the '15, and in particular the comic opera saga of Mar's bullion shipment stranded on the West Sands of St Andrews.

Ironically, the Spanish minister behind the decision to intervene in the British Isles in 1719 was a man who had risen to power in 1715-16 as an exponent of a policy of Anglo-Spanish reconciliation and indeed cooperation. He was also a very remarkable man – Cardinal Guilio Alberoni, the son of an Italian gardener. He had entered the Church and had risen from a humble village curate to a Prince of the Church and first minister of Philip V of Spain. Alberoni had negotiated a commercial treaty with the Hanoverian regime in December 1715. Behind that treaty lay the hope that Hanoverian

Britain could be persuaded to adopt either a friendly, or at least a neutral attitude towards Spanish ambitions in Italy. Part of the peace settlement after the War of the Spanish Succession had involved loss of Spanish territory in Italy. Philip V and Alberoni were determined to recover Sardinia, Sicily, and south Italy. By August 1717 Spanish troops had overrun Sardinia. The Emperor Charles VI of Austria, who had replaced Spain as the ascendant power in the Italian peninsula, was bound to fight back, and Austria was perhaps Britain's most important single European ally. Desperate negotiations in 1717-18 failed to produce a compromise, but did make it clear that British naval power in the Mediterranean was very likely to be placed, in the last analysis, on the Austrian side. British ministers did not want to make a choice, but they could not desert their Austrian ally.

By 1718 Alberoni was committed to an invasion of Sicily, to be followed by a seizure of bridgeheads on the mainland. Though he had risen as an Anglophile, he now started to cast around for ways of neutralising Britain, coming up eventually with an extraordinarily ambitious network of potential allies against Britain and Austria. Apart from Spain, he tried to draw in the Jacobites, Russia, Sweden, and the Turks. The very length of the list shows how slim were his chances of weaving a workable web. His most remarkable proposed addition to the Jacobite-Spanish combination was to be the military might of Sweden. From the days of the great seventeenth-century Swedish king, Gustavus Adolphus, Sweden had risen to great power and had created an extensive Baltic empire. In 1718 a coalition of hostile powers was grappling with Sweden in a successful attempt to strip her of much of her empire, but the Swedes were fighting back with great stubbornness under their king, Charles XII, a great soldier whose blue-coated Swedish infantry and fiery Finnish light cavalry were probably the finest troops in Europe.

As Elector of Hanover, George I was at odds with Sweden because of his determination to incorporate in the electoral dominions two formerly Swedish territories, Bremen and Verden, which would give Hanover a commercially and strategically invaluable grip on the estuaries of the Rivers Weser and Elbe. The two territories had been occupied by Hanoverian troops before Charles XII returned in 1714 from a long exile in Turkey. Thereafter he lead his troops in person in a desperate defence of the fortress of Stralsund, and had enough troubles in dealing with the main armies of his enemies without taking on minor campaigns in Bremen and Verden. In a sense, the Electorate of Hanover was insignificant compared with the Russians and Prussians, whose forces headed the hostile coalition. On the other hand, as rulers of the British Isles the Hanoverians presided over an archipelago whose waters, including those northern waters closest to Sweden, were alive with commercial shipping very vulnerable to well-armed Swedish privateers. By 1715 Swedish attacks had sharply raised insurance premiums on British ships heading for the Baltic. Bailie John Steuart of Inverness suffered with other shipowners, despite his own Jacobite leanings, for privateers were at the best of times insensitive to the finer political distinctions when faced with a chance of snapping up a prize. Steuart remarked sadly in late 1715 that it was much less of a headache to freight a ship southwards for say France 'there being no hazard of Swede privateers that way'. By the spring of 1716 Bailie Steuart had news that one of his ships had been captured in the Kattegat, the narrow waters between northern Denmark and southern Sweden. Late in 1717 he lost another which was going from Inverness to Cork with a cargo of herring and which was picked up by a Swedish privateer off the North Foreland in Kent. It is true that the ships themselves could be bought back at a reasonable rate by sending an agent to the principal Swedish North Sea port, Gothenburg, but the loss of cargo, time and money involved in these captures was serious.

The Royal Navy did not sit idly by. It provided convoy escorts and by 1716 had a squadron in the Baltic under Admiral Norris with orders to cooperate with the Russian and Danish navies against the Swedes. Jacobites in the northern counties of England were not alone in saying that there would soon be a Swedish invasion of Scotland. Jacobites everywhere, with their tendency to clutch at straws to rescue their drowning cause, began to toast 'the gallant Swede', Charles XII. That monarch would seem never to have committed himself to so much as a discussion of how he might possibly assist the Pretender. Jacobites anxious to pull Sweden into their plots just did not grasp that they were in touch only with individual Swedish civil servants and politicians, all of them members of the 'hawk' faction in the Stockholm government, a faction which was resisting a 'dove' faction which wanted to put pressure on Charles XII to end his interminable and unwinnable war. What the 'hawks' wanted was not another war; even they could see they would be lucky to go on fighting the one they had. They wanted money for the war chest of Charles XII and they were not above trying to con some of it out of wealthy British Jacobites. It was all very, very sordid and from the start leaked like a sieve because of the scale of correspondence involved. Apart from their Jacobite victims, the three principal

Swedish figures involved were widely separated. There was the Baron von Görtz, Secretary of State in Stockholm and his two vital overseas contacts, Baron Éric Sparre in Paris, the Swedish ambassador to France, and Count Karl Gyllenborg in London. Lord Stanhope, the leading British minister, and the Earl of Stair, the crafty Scots Whig who was British ambassador in Paris, were able to penetrate the plot partly through agents and partly by tampering with the mails.

The débâcle which followed was triggered off by a blatant breach of diplomatic immunity, probably justified by the antics of the Swedish embassy. General George Wade, an Irishman who was to have a long career as an internal security specialist, military roadbuilder, and rather indifferent field commander, acted as Stanhope's instrument in January 1717 when he presided over the ransacking of the embassy and seizure of Gyllenborg. Under heavy British pressure the Dutch arrested Görtz who was still on their territory. A wave of government propaganda from London made the most of the discomfiture of the deceived Jacobites, and glossed over the unofficial and shapeless nature of Swedish involvement. By 1719 Charles XII had fallen in action, and his successors in power in Sweden were actively cultivating an alliance with Britain.

Part of Alberoni's castle of cards had thus fallen away in January 1717. He was, however, totally committed to the second stage of his Italian offensive. Britain was obliged by the Treaty of Utrecht of 1713 to guarantee the neutrality of Italy. By the Treaty of Westminster, which she had signed with the Emperor in May 1716, she was pledged to maintain the integrity of his dominions, of which Naples was a part. By March 1718 it was clear that affairs were drifting towards war. Early in June, Sir George Byng, who had commanded when the Jacobite invasion force was chased away from the Firth of Forth in 1708, weighed anchor at Spithead to sail to the Mediterranean with a fleet of 20 ships of the line. Despite further attempts at a negotiated settlement, the Spaniards remained intransigent, so on 11 August 1718 Byng attacked and utterly destroyed the main Spanish sleet off Cape Passaro, and thereby rendered any serious Spanish offensive in Italy impractical.

By December the exiled Duke of Ormonde had reached Madrid in response to Spanish approaches. Alberoni, faced with military and political ruin, had decided to lash out at Britain by means of an invasion designed to trigger off a massive Jacobite rising. The cardinal seems to have greatly exaggerated the scale of Jacobite militancy which existed in England, for his plan was originally for an invasion of the West of England, headed by the Tory hero Ormonde. It was confidently asserted that an army of 26,000 could be raised for a march on London. It was in fact Ormonde who argued that there was a case for a diversionary attack on Scotland designed to tie up government forces by raising a rebellion amongst the Highland clans. Asked to name a suitable commander, he suggested the youthful Earl Marischal, a veteran of the '15 now in exile in Paris. At this time nobody envisaged the Scottish rising as any more than a sideshow. It was meant to confuse Westminster and tie up its troops far away from the decisive theatre of war, which in a state as centralised as Britain could only be London. Interestingly, the exiled James Stuart, on whose behalf these risings were to be organised, was not informed about the nature of Ormonde's negotiations until the very start of 1719, when he was not only informed, but asked to come to Spain to associate himself with the expedition.

The main fleet, with about 5,000 Spanish troops aboard, was assembled at Cadiz, while Ormonde waited to join it when it reached Corunna, the principal port of Galicia in north-east Spain. Absolute secrecy was essential for the success of the enterprise, as the Spanish force involved was far too small to have any hope of achieving anything if the British government had the opportunity to take the most minimal of precautions. When the Earl Marischal reached Spain and was interviewed by Alberoni in February 1719, he was promised two frigates, two thousand muskets, and a very small body of Spanish regulars to act as a core for the Army of Jacobite clansmen who were confidently expected to rally to the Pretender's standard. Stair, the well-informed British ambassador in Paris, believed that the funding of the smaller expedition came mainly from the pocket of the Count of Castelblanco, the son-in-law of the Scottish Jacobite Lord Melfort.

The history of the main expedition was one long disaster. Its security cover proved worthless. Alberoni had made the grave mistake of sponsoring a plot against the Regent Orleans of France, with a view to making Philip of Spain Regent of France and of undermining the Anglo-French entente. Lord Stair had no illusions about French public opinion's support for the Jacobites, for religious reasons mainly. He said that 'the byass of all this nation towards the Pretender is inconceivable'. What mattered, however, was that the French government did not share this emotion. Indeed, it made its own sources of information on Spanish doings available to Stair. Westminster knew exactly what was going on as successive delays drove Ormonde to complete despair about his chances. Royal Navy

*7. Castle Fraser, another National Trust property,
perhaps the greatest of a remarkable group
of North-East tower houses*

8. *The Five Sisters of Kintail, one of whose spurs is known as Sgurr nan Spainteach, the Peak of the Spaniards, in memory of the Spanish infantrymen who surrendered on it in 1719*

9. *Kintail, the dramatic setting for the '19,*
now in the care of the National Trust for Scotland

10.

Eilean Donan Castle,
whose
Spanish garrison
surrendered to
the Royal Navy
during the '19

*11. General George Wade, with a military road-building squad at work
on a Highland road in the background (by an unknown artist)*

ships were on patrol off the western approaches to Britain. Several regular regiments moved into the West of England. Four battalions were brought over from Ireland while the Dutch showed their commitment to uphold the Protestant Succession by sending two battalions of Swiss mercenaries to the Thames and three more Dutch battalions to the north of England.

The services of these troops were never called on. As the main Spanish fleet tried to round Cape Finisterre to reach Corunna for its rendezvous with Ormonde and its final reinforcements, it was struck by a terrific gale which raged for forty-eight hours. The flagship was dismasted; the fleet scattered; horses, stores and guns were thrown overboard, and many men died. James Francis Edward Stuart, with characteristic bad luck, reached Corunna on 17 March, after a journey from Madrid, to find the ruins of an expedition straggling into port. James had made an adventurous passage from Rome to Spain, not without hazard from English cruisers in the western Mediterranean. The height of his ambition was to accompany the invasion. That proved physically impossible. By late April Stair had received such reports in Paris as enabled him to write with satisfaction that 'I think we're intirely out of danger from the Spanish invasion for this year'.

Oddly enough, he was wrong. The diversionary force of two frigates had already sailed from Passage, the port of San Sebastian, one of the important coastal cities in the Spanish Basque country. The Earl Marischal had left on 8 March, carrying letters from Ormonde to the Duke of Gordon, MacDonell of Glengarry, Mac-Lean of Brolas, and Donald MacDonald of Benbecula, cousin to Clanranald, letters which of course made much of the invasion of England which would coincide with the arrival of the earl in Scotland. Accompanying the Earl Marischal were detachments of twelve men from each of the twenty-four companies of Don Pedro de Castro's infantry regiment. As the nucleus of a small army, these men were deliberately over-officered, with a lieutenant-colonel, six captains, six lieutenants, and six ensigns, making in all a total of 327 Spanish regulars, conspicuous in their white uniforms with yellow facings. The earl's brother, James Keith, a young man of twenty-two, was not aboard. He crossed into France to warn Scots Jacobites of the opportunity for service presented by the coming invasion.

It is difficult to avoid the conclusion that he would have been better off without some of the personalities who eventually accompanied him from Paris to Scotland. The fundamental problem was factionalism within the Jacobite camp between supporters of the

*Field Marshal James Keith, youngest brother of George Keith,
Earl Marischal. After Sheriffmuir he fled abroad and became
a Field Marshal in the army of Frederick the Great of Prussia*

Duke of Ormonde, and those of the Duke of Mar (for his services in
helping James to lose three crowns, Mar had been elevated to ducal
rank in the phantom Jacobite peerage). Campbell of Glendaruel, the
leading Jacobite contact in Paris, and General Dillon, who had been
left at St Germains as the Pretender's represenative in France, were
of Mar's faction. Worse still, Glendaruel had his own tame Highland

magnate in the shape of the Marquess of Tullibardine, the amiable but weak and disinherited heir of Atholl. At some point in 1717 when exaggerated hopes of a Swedish alliance were flying around in Jacobite circles, James had issued a commission making Tullibardine commander of all his forces in Scotland, and that commission was in Tullibardine's pocket when he embarked with the unsuspecting James Keith. A much more useful companion was William Mackenzie, Earl of Seaforth, the chief of a mighty clan in the northwest Highlands, the designated area for the attempted rising. James Keith had met other Jacobite personalities like General Gordon at Rouen on his way north, and had left funds for them to hire ships for Scotland. General Gordon was too ill for the journey, but Lochiel and MacDonald of Clanranald did make the crossing with Keith, Tullibardine, and Glendaruel.

Leaving Le Havre in a small ship which was nearly captured by the Royal Navy as it sailed round the west of Ireland, James Keith reached the Isle of Lewis to find that his elder brother's two ships were at anchor in Stornoway. There a council of war showed deep division among the leaders. The Earl Marischal, as senior Jacobite major-general present, urged a landing on the mainland and a dash on Inverness, where he understood the garrison to be a weak one of 300 men. Such a coup would encourage support, as well as supplying a base where the Jacobites could hold out pending the arrival of Ormonde. Wiser far in their innate defeatism, Tullibardine and Glendaruel were all for remaining in Lewis until they had definite information about Ormonde's landing in England. Had Ormonde's squadron ever reached England's home waters, it would probably have been destroyed by the waiting Royal Navy. Had he managed to land, his troops, many of whom had been pressganged into uniform shortly before embarkation, would probably have been crushed by the superior professional forces waiting to repulse an invasion. There was little justification for the puny Jacobite expedition in Scotland crossing to the mainland until it heard that Ormonde had landed and scored at least a provisional success.

After passionate debates, in the course of which Tullibardine suddenly tabled his Commander-in-Chief Scotland commision, a typical committee compromise was reached. Tullibardine was accepted as the military commander, despite general lack of confidence in his capacity, and he agreed to implement the Earl Marischal's strategy, despite the fact that he did not believe in it. After being blown back and fore across the stormy waters of the Minch between the Outer Hebrides and Seaforth's country of Kintail on the mainland, the Jac-

*Two anti-Jacobite medals showing the fate of traitors
and the futility of Jacobite aspirations*

obites were glad to make a landfall not in Kintail, but on the shores
of Loch Alsh, the narrow waters between the south-eastern tip of
the Isle of Skye and that part of the mainland immediately to the
north. They soon received news that the Lowland Jacobites, despite
the usual barrage of hysterically optimistic reports designed to
pitchfork them into premature commitment, were determined not
to budge until they had hard news that Ormonde had established a
bridgehead in the west of England. The steady spirit and clear mind
of the Jacobite MP George Lockhart of Carnwath set the tone of the
Lowland response. He was emphatic that repeal of the Act of Union
had to be the main plank in the Jacobite platform, and that there had
to be something better than unconfirmed rumours about Ormonde
before Lowland gentlemen risked their lives and inheritances by
rising in rebellion.

Meanwhile the Jacobite army had selected as its base an old
Mackenzie stronghold, the romantic Eilean Donan Castle situated
on a small island at the point where Loch Alsh divides into Loch
Long and Loch Duich. Strategically, it was Loch Duich which mattered, for it led straight to the mouth of Glen Shiel, a striking glen
with the peaks of the Five Sisters of Kintail on its northern side.
More relevant in 1719 was the fact that from Glen Shiel ran a route
into Glen Moriston, a glen whose river runs into Loch Ness, the long
stretch of deep water which in turn enabled a force in small boats to
land within a mile or two of Inverness. Here was the only west-east

route which would permit the Earl Marischal's plan to be implemented, for it depended entirely on speed and surprise. Tullibardine, however, felt, probably correctly, that the most intelligent move under the circumstances was speedy re-embarkation for Spain. Marischal, superseded as land commander, was still in command of the ships. He therefore ordered the two frigates home. His aim was to force his companions to advance and conquer or die. Most did neither.

They were in fact caught in a Hanoverian pincer. From the sea came a Royal Navy squadron of five warships which proceeded very efficiently to knock out Eilean Donan, where a garrison of 45 Spaniards guarded the bulk of the Jacobite ammunition and supplies. As long ago as 1685 Argyll's rebellion against James VII and II had been seriously hampered by the same tactical folly of storing weapons and munitions in an offshore castle in the presence of an enemy with total naval supremacy. On 10 May 1719 Captain Boyle led three warships close enough to batter the castle with their broadsides, and after a fierce bombardment, a couple of boatloads of British tars were enough to secure the surrender of some very dazed Spaniards. Meanwhile the other jaw of the pincer began to close as the Hanoverian Major-General Wightman, a veteran of Sheriffmuir, prepared to march out of Inverness in the opposite direction to that proposed by the more hawkish Jacobites. Loch Ness, Glen Moriston, and Glen Shiel, could serve the needs of a vigorous defence as well as those of a surprise attack. Very early in June Wightman marched out with a much reinforced Inverness garrison. He had some 850 regular infantry, 120 dragoons, 130 Highlanders, and a battery of four light bronze field mortars called cohorns after their inventor the Dutch siege specialist Baron van Cohorn.

To oppose him, the cornered Jacobites had disappointingly few troops, not least because it was by June common knowledge in the Highlands that Ormonde's expedition was a fiasco. James Keith remarked that 'Not above a thousand men appeared, and even those seemed not very fond of the enterprise'. Lochiel came up from Cameron country in Lochaber with only 150 men. Seaforth, in his own country, did better with 500. Lord George Murray, Tullibardine's younger brother, came in with some men from Perthshire. Another Jacobite veteran of the '15 arrived in the shape of the irrepressible Rob Roy MacGregor. Rob had eeled his way out of the last rising by a very nominal surrender to Campbell of Fonab, a doughty warrior who had fought and defeated Spaniards in Panama, but who was widely accused of letting Rob off because he might be of future use to Argyll. On 10 June the Jacobite army stood to fight about five miles up the glen from Invershiel and in an enormously strong position on the hillsides, commanding a small bridge over the River Shiel. They had even thrown up such entrenchments as the rocky ground permitted. In numbers the two small armies were evenly matched. Wightman had many fewer Highlanders but they proved invaluable as guides through the mountains, and they fought with conviction for they were men from the staunchly Whig Clan Munro led by Captain George Munro of Culcairn, younger brother of Sir Robert Munro of Foulis. Wightman seized the initiative, advancing up the slopes after a sharp mortar barrage. For three hours the infantry kept up a fierce fire fight, with intermittent charges with cold steel and a free use of grenades by Wightman's crack grenadier units. Roughly a hundred men were killed or wounded on each side, but the moral victory lay with the Hanoverians, whose pugnacious tactics broke the will of the Jacobite rankers. By evening the Jacobite army was in full retreat. The next day, with no arms, provision, or hope, its leaders decided to flee, urging their Highlanders to disband, and the Spaniards, who would be treated as prisoners of war, to surrender.

Eighteenth-century conventions between regular forces normally ensured rapid repatriation of prisoners whom the victor preferred not to have to feed. Westminster in fact simply refused to pay anything for the captives beyond their regular Spanish pay, and demanded, not without a certain logic, that the Spaniards refund not only that but also their repatriation costs. Borrowing from their captors, and sustained by the charity of Jacobite supporters when they reached Edinburgh, the 274 Spanish prisoners were finally saved from their absurd but painful position when their commander received bills of exchange from the Spanish ambassador in Holland sufficient to clear their debts and finance their voyage home. By December 1719 Cardinal Alberoni had fallen from power in Spain and was an exile in Italy.

By then James Francis Edward Stuart was also back in Italy after Spanish ministers had made it clear to him that they thought he had outstayed his welcome in Spain. In Rome he could count on safe refuge for he was cherished by a succession of Popes, whom he called 'my landlords'. He also enjoyed many friendships among the College of Cardinals. The Roman Church cherished James partly for his own unaffected piety, partly for his potential importance as a Catholic claimant for the British thrones. As the latter, it was imperative he should marry to beget heirs. Early in 1718 the Duke of

*Jacobite medal celebrating the birth of
Prince Charles Edward Stewart in December 1719.
The globe shows the three kingdoms claimed by his father
and the pillar symbolises the dynasty*

Ormonde and Charles Wogan, an Irish Jacobite who had escaped
from Newgate Jail after the '15, had picked a bride for him in the
nubile fifteen-year-old shape of Maria Clementina Sobieska, grand-
daughter of King John Sobieski of Poland and also a descendant of
the imperial Hapsburgs. Apart from her child-bearing potential,
Clementina appealed to an exiled court short of cash, because she
offered to alleviate that problem with her dowry of family jewellery.

After an adventurous trip to Italy, which included arrest by her
Austrian kinsman the Emperor (now very much allied to Hanove-
rian England) and an escape organised by the practised hand of
Wogan, Clementina eventually married James at Montefiascone, at

the odd hour of midnight on 1 September 1719. The marriage was a political and personal disaster. Politically James had suffered by being compelled to accept Papal protection. That was why British diplomats had helped hound him out of France and Lorraine. They wanted to identify the Pretender with an alien Counter-Reformation culture. Clementina, with her Polish background, merely widened the deep gulf between the mental world of the exiled court and British attitudes, even the attitudes of most British Jacobites. Then again, if James was rapidly becoming an unsuccessful bore, Clementina became a fully-fledged neurotic. They produced two worthwhile achievements together. One, born in 1720, was Prince Charles, the other Prince Henry who was born in 1725 and whose godfather was Pope Benedict XIII. Jacobitism had a future, however dim.

CHAPTER VI

Between the '19 and the '45

BY THE YEAR 1720 IT WOULD NOT HAVE BEEN unreasonable to argue that the only disaster which the exiled Stuarts had managed to avoid was genetic suicide. There was at least the infant heir, Prince Charles. Between 1710 and 1719 the Jacobite cause had experienced political, military and moral catastrophe. The farce of the '19, where the Jacobite invasions were clearly mere tools of an alien and hostile European power, was the last straw, undermining what little political credibility James had as an alternative regime in England. The Battle of Glen Shiel had been well fought by both sides. The Spanish and British regulars did their job, in a professional fashion, and the Jacobite Highlanders, who stood the mortar bombs, grenades, and musketry of the Hanoverian forces for three hours, showed extraordinary staunchness. This was all the more remarkable since most of them were well-informed enough and intelligent enough to grasp what a mess their leaders had made of the situation.

James himself rather lost heart as the 1720s ground on, and by the 1730s he could scarcely be regarded as an active Jacobite. Sir Robert Walpole, British prime minister after 1720, completely penetrated the formal structure of Jacobitism with an expensive but effective espionage system. A hopeless Jacobite plot concocted by Francis Atterbury, High Church and Tory Bishop of Rochester, in 1722-23, ended in Atterbury's flight to the Continent. Mar became a Hanoverian pensioner. Bolingbroke made his peace with George I and returned to his estates, though not the House of Lords, in 1724. In 1726 Seaforth followed his example, and showed by his subsequent behaviour in 1745 that he meant to keep his word and shun all future Jacobite plotting.

And yet the cause of the exiled dynasty did not die. Its survival as a part of political culture in Britain owed almost nothing to the mini-court pursuing its own fitful obsessions in Rome. Contact with it on the part of 'Country' Jacobites was usually just a mistake, even for so devoted and saintly a figure as Alexander fourth and last Lord Forbes of Pitsligo. This remarkable Episcopalian mystic, educated in France, had boycotted the Scots Parliament after a dignified protest against the proposed Act of Union in 1705. He was one of the very few equally active in the '15 and the '45. An eight-month spell at the Jacobite court in Rome in 1719 simply led to quarrels with the Jacobite Secretary of State, James Murray, and to Pitsligo withdrawing with characteristic dignity but very much under the displeasure of James. Jacobitism survived because of developments in Britain, and more particularly in Scotland, where the Hanoverian regime was committed to destroying its social and ideological base.

In practice the Westminster government made a hopelessly ineffective stab at the task, though its failure owed much to obstruction by others. Forfeiture of Jacobite estates is the classic example. This was the normal response of any early-modern European government to a noble-led rebellion. Once a man was attainted and convicted of high treason it was in theory possible under the draconian English law of treason (extended to Scotland after the abortive '08), to strip his family of the landed property which was the key to power, and transfer it to the well-affected. In the eighteenth, as in the twentieth century, however, if Westminster reached out too harshly for legal power to crush its critics, it was liable to find judges and juries reluctant to convict. That was what happened after the '15. Scottish society was dominated by the landed classes. The Advocates who pled before the central courts in Edinburgh and the judges with judicial peerages who sat on their benches were nearly all lairds whose conservative souls rebelled at the very idea of forfeiture of heritable estates.

Commissioners were appointed by statute to deal with the forfeitures. They decided to divide into two bodies — one for England and Ireland and one for Scotland. There was only a limited amount of Irish business as the Anglican aristocracy of Ireland had not offered James much support. The English forfeitures went roughly according to plan, though even here the Commissioners complained of organised attempts to sabotage the forcible sale of the goods of traitors. A whole layer of old-fashioned Tory Jacobites was removed from certain areas of the north of England to be replaced by aggressive Whig men on the make, often capitalist landlords with a big stake in coal mining. With the introduction of the steam engine to solve problems of deep drainage, this group of men went on to forge a new ascendancy, while the Roman Catholic population of Lancashire drew the logical conclusion that the best course for it in any future Jacobite rebellion was to keep a low profile until the issue was decided. Between Whig assertion and Catholic passivity, the northern parts of England were to be a poor recruiting ground for Prince Charles in the '45.

The 'Commissioners Appointed to Enquire of the Estates of certain Traitors in that Part of Great Britain called Scotland' had a much less happy time of it. They found that the Scottish judges meant to obstruct their proceedings on a wide range of grounds. The Scottish Barons of the Exchequer, for example, who carried prime responsibility for financial disputes between the Crown and its subjects, managed to raise charges against a large number of men of note involved in the rebellion. The charges related to a relatively minor lapse which these men had committed before the rebellion proper, and by ordering sheriffs to take control of their estates to secure payment of mild fines, the Barons made it difficult for the Forfeited Estates Commissioners to get control of these properties.

The Court of Session, the highest Scottish civil court, proved even more obstructive. It was only too ready to entertain a barrage of claims by people who said they were creditors owed money by men liable to forfeiture for their part in the rebellion. This was a shrewd exploitation of one of the basic facts about forfeiture: no government could afford not to recognise, and arrange payment of, the legitimate debts outstanding on a property it intended to forfeit. The debtors usually greatly outnumbered the proprietorial family, so failure to pay them risked the alienation of large numbers of people. Yet the rulings of the Court of Session clearly went well beyond mere prudence. Sir John Carnegie of Pitarrow was in July 1716 appointed factor on the estates of the Earl of Southesk, a notable rebel. Pitarrow was appointed by the Court of Session as guardian of the interest not of the state but of totally unspecified debts allegedly owed to a group of creditors who included a couple of Lords of Session. Zealous Whigs pointed out that Pitarrow was a notorious and open Jacobite, with a particular taste for harrying Presbyterian ministers. Stirling of Keir's estates were handed over to the factorship of his own steward, Walter Stirling, who had also been an active Jacobite. Many loyal Jacobite stewards were thus appointed, though the most thoughtful allocation of a factorship by the Lords of Session was probably that over the estate of the Earl of Carnwath. Their Lordships appointed Carnwath's mother.

Law in early modern Britain could be savage, but it was also part of the public theatre of government, and it could display an eccentric life of its own. Lawyers displayed a fanatical regard for the precise forms of law, often to the point of ignoring the substance of a case. For example, the slightest error in the form of an indictment or attainder, even when it was for high treason, could lead to a patently guilty prisoner being set free. This was a not infrequent occurrence under English common law, and it happened in Scotland in 1716. General Gordon of Auchintoul and Farquharson of Inverey were attainted under wrong Christian names, which led the judges to rule that the attainders were invalid, despite the very conspicuous rebellion of both men. Some noble Jacobites, such as Lord Pitsligo, were not even attainted. It is true that the great speculative boom in England known as the South Sea Bubble did throw up a company which chose to speculate in forfeited Jacobite estates. Because it chose to use the legal framework provided by a former privileged but superannuated company, it had the unlikely title of the Company of Undertakers for raising the Thames water in York Buildings. It bought Scottish and northern English forfeited Jacobite properties on a large scale in the 1720s, but was virtually bankrupt by the late 1730s, and very vulnerable to the sort of pressures which made it give a lease of the forfeited Fingask estate to a certain Mr Hume, otherwise known as the Jacobite Sir David Thriepland of Fingask. One way or another, the impact of forfeiture on Scotland after the '15 was severely blunted.

Certain groups of people were marked out for punishment by their blatant Jacobitism in 1715-16. Episcopal clergymen were a case in point. As a group, they had stuck their necks out, fully confirming the charges of their Presbyterian opponents. After the failure of the '15 some thirty Episcopal clergy were ejected from their livings in Aberdeenshire. These usually scholarly and sometimes saintly men had nearly all accepted toleration under Queen Anne by swearing an Act of Abjuration of the Pretender, for whom they had all then preached and prayed during the rising. Whether their inevitable expulsion from their pulpits did the Hanoverian cause a great deal of good in the medium term may be doubted. Their parishioners resented clumsy interference by a disliked government, and the ministers themselves often set up as tutors or schoolmasters, instilling a heady brew of Jacobite ideology into the heads of the young gentlemen of the region who officered Jacobite regiments in the '45. The wisest policy for the new Presbyterian regime was in many ways to wait for a Jacobite incumbent to die and then try to secure the succession. That gentle Jacobite, Robert Kirk, minister of

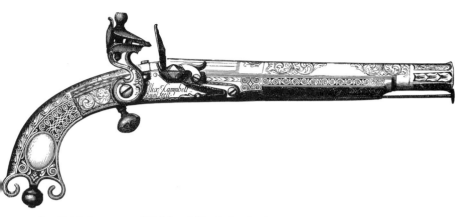

*A mid-18th-century Highland flintlock pistol
with a ram's horn butt made by Alexander Campbell in Doune*

Balquhidder and Aberfoyle, Gaelic scholar and authority on the fair-
ies (on whom he wrote an admirable book), was allowed simply to
fade away, though whether into a grave or into a fairy hill is still a
matter of some controversy. Many a Whig must have wished that
some of the more pugnacious Aberdeenshire Jacobite clergy would
also depart for a Celtic never-never land.

The Westminster government did have plans for dealing with the
heart of the Scottish Jacobite problem — the Jacobite Highlands. Its
first step was to pass a Disarming Act, but the result of such legislation was depressingly predictable: the Whig clans did surrender
weapons, while the Jacobite ones either refused or surrendered old
and broken ones. The very sensible Commander-in-Chief Scotland
after the '19, General George Carpenter, provided his political
masters with a realistic assessment of the situation. He argued that
the defeat of the '19 had made precious little difference to Highland
realities. His lumbering regular troops could only move freely in the
summer. They had no capacity whatever to catch fleet-footed young
Highlanders most of whom would in any case be living in the huts
called shielings in the high hill pastures to which the cattle moved
every summer. It was therefore impossible to disarm Jacobite areas.
Only the landlord had the power to force tenants to surrender con-
cealed weapons. He could do this by simple terrorism — destroying
the houses and seizing the cattle and crops of recalcitrants at a
season when such action was virtually a sentence of death. Of
course, this was the last thing any committed Jacobite landlord-chief
would do.

Meanwhile up at the northern end of the Great Glen, that diagonal geological rift through the central area of the Highlands from Fort William to Inverness, Simon Fraser of Lovat was pondering and offering, as was his wont, unsolicited advice to the government. Simon had puffed relentlessly his own part in the recapture of Inverness by the Whigs in the latter part of the '15. It was an almost bloodless operation, but in Simon's version it closely resembled one of the battles of Alexander the Great. In 1724 Simon Fraser sat in Castle Dounie near Inverness brooding over how to make the Highlands a more profitable place for Simon Fraser of Lovat, to whom he felt the defeat of the '15 was largely due. The result of his deliberations was a memorandum to King George I 'concerning the State of the Highlands'. It is an interesting document which discusses intelligently the distinctive culture and the clan structure of Gaelic society. Its obsessive theme, however, was the problem of law and order in a region plagued by theft, especially of such movable wealth as cattle, and where blackmail had become a significant industry, with its own outstanding entrepreneurs such as Rob Roy MacGregor. Rob did offer a service, in the sense that he protected clients from other thieves and tried to recover any goods stolen from them, but he did encourage subscriptions by practical demonstrations of the misfortunes which might befall non-subscribers.

Lovat's memorandum quite rightly pointed out that the recent Disarming Act had merely weakened the position of government loyalists in the Highlands. Due to extreme political instability in the region, the Westminster government had been unwilling to continue a system whereby policing in the Highlands was operated at least partially through independent companies of troops raised by local gentry for local service at government expense. These independent companies had, as Lovat pointed out, functioned under King William but had eventually been disbanded for fear that they might turn on the regime which funded them. To cut a long tale short, Lovat more or less advised the government to make him an active Justice of the Peace (another neglected policing appointment in the Highlands); the commander of an independent company; and preferably Lord Lieutenant of Inverness-shire. Privately, it was Lovat's conviction that the least the government could do for him was to add him also to their list of Representative Peers for Scotland, a list which was always returned by the needy and subservient Scots peerage at nominal elections.

The government had the wit to distinguish between the shrewd comment and the egregious self-interest in the memorandum.

[In a private collection]

A Highland laird, Robert Grant of Lurg, with his ram's horn pistol

Instead of heaping the slippery Simon with offices, George I on 3 July 1724 ordered General Wade to proceed to the Highlands and report on the matters raised by Lovat. He reported in December 1724, starting with an estimate of the military capacity of the Highlands. He reckoned that they could produce 22,000 fighting men, of whom a maximum of 10,000 were well-affected to the Hanoverian regime. The rest were Jacobites who had made a nonsense of the 1716 Disarming Act, in connection with which Wade swore that 'great Quantities of broken and useless Arms were brought from Holland and delivered up to the Persons appointed to receive the same at exorbitant prices'. He agreed that independent companies were far more suitable than regular troops for police work in the Highlands, and recommended their resurrection, though he cannily added that one reason they had been supressed was that their dishonest commanders seldom kept more than half their nominal roll of men under arms, whilst pocketing the pay for every name on the roll. Wade urged the development and improvement of a system of forts and outposts in the central part of the Highlands. He argued that in such a network the positions of strength could only be made mutually reinforcing if road and water communication between the forts were improved. He agreed that independent companies of Highlanders commanded by Gaelic-speaking officers were essential for effective policing and internal security. Finally, he urged the appointment of an adequate cadre of Sheriffs, Deputy Sheriffs, and Justices of the Peace in the Highlands. By the summer of 1725 Wade was in Scotland with a commission as Commander of the Forces in North Britain. He had asked for funds to repair the defences of Edinburgh Castle and Fort William; to build a suitable vessel to dominate and use Loch Ness; to build two new forts and barracks at Inverness and 'Killiehuimen' (later known as Fort Augustus); and to develop the roads between the garrisons.

In the years before he relinquished his Scottish command in 1740, Wade achieved a fair proportion of the programme he had set himself. His plans to develop a sequence of forts along the Great Glen had been anticipated by Cromwell in the seventeenth century, but the Cromwellian citadel at Inverness had been dismantled after the Restoration. Wade's Inverness fort was built on Castle Hill beside the River Ness, a glacial mound or drumlin composed of very loose sand and gravel dumped by retreating ice. Called Fort George*, the new structure looked stronger than it was, as the events of the '45 showed. Wade constructed a sixty-ton galley armed with half a dozen light cannon called 'patteroes' (from a Spanish word denoting a light anti-personnel piece which had originally fired a scatter of stones). Its job was to ply Loch Ness to link Fort George with his next fort. The varied spellings of what is now Fort Augustus go back to Gaelic 'Cill Chuimein' meaning the church of Cummein, a seventh-century Celtic saint. There had been an earlier fort on the site by 1716, but Wade reckoned it was too far from Loch Ness, so he rebuilt it beside a harbour for the galley on the River Tarff. It was a stout building only completed in 1742, but vulnerable,

---

* A name later transferred to a much stronger fort north-east of Inverness

*12. Scotstarvit, a traditional tower house; the Scots of
Scotstarvit later built a Georgian mansion, Hill of Tarvit;
both are now owned by the National Trust for Scotland*

13. A painting by Harold Wylie of the action between L'ELISABETH and HMS LYON which enabled Prince Charles to continue his voyage to Scotland aboard the LE DU TEILLAY in 1745

*The first Fort George (1744), built by General George Wade
(from an engraving by Paul Sandby)*

as the siege of February 1746 demonstrated. Fort William, bits of
which had a bad habit of falling down, was upgraded by Wade and
was the only Highland fort to repay his efforts. On the approach to
the Great Glen, Wade built Ruthven Barracks on another spectacu-
larly exposed mound, which had already carried two previous castles, just over the Spey from Kingussie. On the far side of his central
line he created the small post of Bernera Barracks in Glenelg, to
control a route to Skye. Like Ruthven, it fell in the '45.

To link his garrisons with one another and with the Lowlands,
Wade built the roads and bridges which were undoubtedly his greatest claim to long-term fame. His greatest single road was the one
from Inverness to Dunkeld. Like all the others it was built by detachments of soldiers under the command of their own officers, with a
certain amount of specialist help on such matters as surveying and
bridge-building. In July 1728 Wade reported that

'I am now with all possible diligence carrying on the new road for
wheel-carriages between Dunkeld and Inverness, of about 80
English measured miles'

The average cost of his roads seems to have been approximately
£70 per mile. He had perhaps the greatest difficulty with the final

stage of his important road along the Great Glen from Fort William to Inverness, as it required a lot of blasting to build his preferred route on the east side of Loch Ness. With strategic sense, but in defiance of topography, Wade built an alternative route through the central Highlands, from Aberfeldy to Dalnacardoch, where it joined his Inverness road. At Dalwhinnie another Wade road struck west and climbed over the Pass of Corrieyairack by a series of dizzy zigzags reaching a height of over 2,500 feet before plunging down again towards Fort Augustus.

On few topics do people tend to have more misleading impressions than on General Wade's roads. First, it must be said that they were not the first roads in the Highlands. The idea that Highland society was so 'primitive' as not to need roads is simply absurd. There had, for example, been a road through the central Grampians since the end of the thirteenth century. It was formed by a Comyn Earl of Atholl and Badenoch to link his two castles of Blair Atholl and Ruthven. This is a notably direct route. The modern variant by Drumochter is a distance of 42 miles. Comyn's Road was 27 miles long, and even it had been superseded, probably by the sixteenth century, by an even shorter route through the Minigaig Pass, which cut off another $1\frac{1}{2}$ miles. Once a traveller reached Blair Atholl in the seventeenth century, he could carry on down the Garry-Tummel-Tay Valley, which is the line of the modern road, or he could take at least two other, now long disused, roads eastward to Strathardle — the Shinagag Road and the Glen Loch Road. The latter lies at the foot of the Beinn a' Ghlo mountain range in a glen devoted to sheep and shooting, but in the eighteenth century anyone perched on the shoulder of Carn Liath would have seen the Glen Loch Road as a link between a succession of clachans or clusters of houses.

These were not all-weather roads. That was the crucial difference between them and more modern roads. Highlanders travelled in the dry season, except in emergencies. In winter they stayed at home or visited neighbouring clachans. Only in the summer would they want to move great quantities of wealth by land and that took the form of herds of black cattle which needed rights of way known as 'drove roads' rather than roads as the term is to be understood in the twentieth century. Wade's roads were all-weather routes for moving troops. Neither the lines nor the gradients which he accepted were necessarily suitable for future commercial traffic. Some of his roads are indeed the basis of modern lines of communication. Others are unused, etched into hillsides (where they tended to be dug in rather than excavated out), and long greened-over. Wade's roads do represent a great achievement of construction. Originally built without bridges and relying like their predecessors mainly on fords, they were in due course enhanced by some fine bridges at key points, of which perhaps the best-known is the bridge over the Tay at Aberfeldy designed by the architect William Adam, who was appointed Mason to the Board of Ordnance in North Britain in 1730. Wade himself, made a full general in 1739, had left Scotland in 1740, but the road programme continued under his successor General Clayton.

Indeed, military road-building continued long after the '45, until in the late eighteenth century there was a reaction against the construction costs and recurrent charges for that high proportion of the system which was no longer seen as a military necessity. The paradox is that Wade's system of forts and roads viewed as a security system proved a total fiasco the one time it was ever put to the test. The only army which made extensive and successful use of General Wade's roads was the Jacobite army of Prince Charles in the '45.

The explanation for this paradox was military and political. Wade's road construction might have achieved its purpose had his vision of an adequate garrison and policing force been adhered to. It was not. Wade always assumed that a significant force of regulars supplemented by irregulars organised in independent Highland companies would be necessary to hold the Highlands in a firm grip. He was himself more of a heavy-handed policeman than a battlefield soldier. In 1725 he had led a very large punitive column of horse, foot, artillery, and government lawyers to crush the city of Glasgow which was rioting against the imposition of a new Malt Tax. This tax was seen as not only unfair as between Scotland and England but also a gross breach of the Act of Union. Feeling was running so high against the imposition of the new tax in other Scottish burghs, not least Edinburgh, that there was a danger of Westminster having to face a meaningful challenge to its claim to arbitrary power unfettered by any document such as the Act of Union. By making an example of Glasgow, Wade had crushed the crisis in the bud.

Highlanders were not as vulnerable or as static as Glasgow burgesses. Wade needed light troops to handle them. In April 1725 orders were issued for the raising of six independent companies. The first three, each 114 strong, were commanded by Grant of Ballindalloch, Fraser of Lovat, and Campbell of Lochnell. The other three companies, each commanded by an impeccably Whig gentleman, were only 71 strong. Each Highland fort had a resident group of 30 Highlanders to act as scouts. By 1729 these men were being paid as regulars, and in 1739 four additional companies were raised. The history of the independent companies was not altogether happy. Lovat in particular proved difficult and devious. Wade suspected him not just of crypto-Jacobitism but also of the classic independent company commander's ploy of sending at least half his men home whilst pocketing their pay. Simon, paranoid at the best of times, rapidly persuaded himself that there was a deliberate plot against him and his rage when he was eventually deprived of his company knew no bounds. In any case, by the late 1730s Britain was drifting into war with Spain and the British government simply could not resist the temptation to see in the independent companies another reservoir of cannon-fodder for overseas service.

The letters of service issued in October 1739 ordering the expansion of the six existing companies to ten also ordered that all the companies be formed into a new regular unit commanded by John Earl of Crawford. Numbered the 43rd Regiment (later 42nd), its officers' commissions were dated October 1739 and it has always been known as the Black Watch after the dark government-issue tartan of its kilts. The men were recruited on the specific understanding that they were to serve in Scotland. By 1742 Westminster had resolved on a breach of trust, for it decoyed the regiment south to London with a cock-and-bull story of His Majesty's anxiety to review his faithful Highlanders in person. Then it was intended to ship the men to Flanders. Rumours were soon flying around the regiment that they might be shipped to the tropical graveyard of the West Indies. The upshot was a mutiny justified so far as any resistance to tyranny can be justified, but crushed with several executions. When George II's younger son the Duke of Cumberland led the British infantry forward into the butcher's yard of the Battle of Fontenoy in May 1745, the Black Watch was in his line of battle.

Meanwhile home security in Scotland was left in the hands of the senile Lieutenant-General Joshua Guest, well into his ninth decade and with virtually no troops to defend the Lowlands or police the Highlands. The fact that there was little face of a government in the Highlands proved of small consequence in normal times. Central governments cling to the theory that without their presence their subject provinces would dissolve in anarchy, but in 1744 the Highlands were making an excellent job of governing themselves, partly through their web of heritable jurisdictions, and partly through new arrangements. As the cattle industry expanded, effective policing of drove routes for the herds on their way to market became a vital matter for most Chiefs. On 13 October 1744 at Keppoch an agreement was reached between Alexander MacDonell of Keppoch, John MacDonell of Glengarry, and Donald Cameron Younger of Lochiel. To provide for the prevention of crime among their dependents and the suppression of raiding, these Chiefs pledged mutual cooperation in a document solemnly lodged with 'Sir Alexander McDonal of McDonald Baronet', and they appointed gentlemen of their clans as deputies for various districts. Keppoch appointed Ranald Mac-Donell of Aberarder for the Braes of Badenoch, and in the Braes of Lochaber he named his brother Donald, with Donald MacDonell of Tirnadris, Donald MacDonell of Cranachan, and Alexander Mac-Donell of Tulloch. Various chiefs became active law-and-order entrepreneurs, offering the services of a private watch of armed men, in exchange for an annual fee. Nobody was more active in that field in 1744 than Ewen Macpherson Younger of Cluny, whose watch service spanned the Grampian Highlands. Only a bolt from the blue could have shattered the pattern of an evolving Highland society, but that was exactly what was coming.

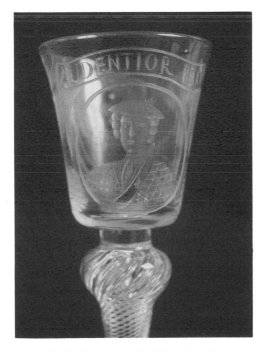

An 18th-century Jacobite wine glass

CHAPTER VII

The '45

THOUGH JACOBITISM WAS A POLITICAL SUB-CULTURE with a life of its own, most people, including most committed Jacobites, had pretty well written off any chance of further rebellion by the 1730s. The High Church Jacobites of the Church of England had been systematically suppressed by the Whig regime at Westminster, and of course the patronage at the disposal of the Crown enabled its ministers to dilute the body of disaffected clergy with more and more safe Whigs. Then the débâcle of Bishop Atterbury's plot in the early 1720s effectively beheaded Anglican Jacobitism. One reason why the English Jacobite rising in 1715 had been so half-hearted and indecisive was the distress and embarrassment of its Anglican leadership when it discovered that it was leading a rising which was almost entirely Roman Catholic in personnel. Anglican and Roman Catholic Jacobites did not have a good relationship. High Anglicans, and especially those of the extreme Non-Juring persuasion who had refused the oaths of allegiance to William III, were by definition passionate believers in an Anglican church-state. Their leading propagandists, such as Charles Leslie, kept urging the Old Pretender to embrace Anglicanism, not because it was expedient, but because it was right. Though James had in fact in 1702 pledged himself to secure the Church of England in its privileges and liberties, and to surrender royal ecclesiastical patronage to a committee of bishops, he could not escape from the basic dilemma. Nor did the Roman Catholics of England offer any real power-base after 1716. They were Jacobite, but they had taken such a hammering in the aftermath of the '15 that they had no stomach for active rebellion.

The very nature of Jacobite ideology tended to endorse a passive approach on the part of its adherents. They cultivated a ritual year, with celebrations of the Pretender's birthday, and they treasured Jacobite keepsakes and engraved glasses, but fundamentally they had a mystical belief — well expressed in the scaffold speeches of Jacobite martyrs — that their dynasty represented a Right Moral Order. Its restoration to the British thrones was therefore a matter of cosmic justice. By definition such a restoration would solve all the tensions and troubles which alarmed their conservative souls when they looked round the British scene. The fact that it would have had no such effect — it would have solved some problems and created others — is neither here nor there. They believed in the redemptive nature of their sacral king with total conviction. Yet that conviction could easily turn into a calm expectation of the repeat of the 'miracle' of 1660, when the Stuarts, against all the odds, came back to rule, without themselves having to do anything very much. People, in Jacobite terms, came to their senses and realised God wanted them to respect His annointed royal line. Actually the Stuarts came back in 1660 because, after two years of frantic search for almost any alternative, none could be found. After 1688 there was a very real alternative with its own aggressive ideology, perhaps best expressed in Sir John Thornhill's vast baroque painting in the Great Hall of Greenwich Hospital. Completed in 1717 it is an apotheosis of the Protestant Succession, seen as a great English nationalist triumph, trampling on the forces of Popery and arbitrary power.

More aggressive Jacobites hoped for a re-run of 1688, with the landing of a substantial foreign professional army to neutralise the large standing army at the disposal of the Whig regime. This was a very sensible attitude. A society like England with a totally centralised higher political system was no place for half-hearted provincial revolts, especially against a warrior dynasty from Germany with a large professional army and a clique of ministers who would defend their own powers until the enemy was literally pounding on the doors of Westminster Hall. English treason law deliberately made rebellion an all-or-nothing game. The stakes were too high for any responsible gentleman of substance to be keen on rising without a fair chance of success.

France alone had the power to intervene in England on a scale sufficient to restore the Stuarts. This fact of life had been underlined by the fiasco of Spanish intervention in 1719. Everyone knew that the Old Pretender's hopes hinged on a French invasion, and James ordered his followers to do all they could to embroil France and England. Of cultural antipathy between the two states there was plenty, but the long period of empirical Anglo-French cooperation after the '15 blasted what little hope was left in informed Jacobite circles. Even Whigs began to regard the Pretender as an interesting curiosity rather than as a real menace. When the poet Thomas Gray, author of the 'Elegy written in a Country Churchyard', visited Rome in 1740, he went to a ball specifically to catch a glance of 'The Pretender'. He made no bones about the fact that in appearance James was 'a good deal resembling King James the Second', so the old falsehood of the child smuggled into the palace was no longer necessary. Gray thought James looked pathetic and said that he lived in a mini-court dominated by Lord Dunbar and a few 'Scotch lords', who he claimed 'would be very glad to make their peace at home'.

Quite a few leading Jacobite exiles had indeed made their peace with the British government. The most significant Scottish example was the Earl of Seaforth who came to terms with King George in 1726. He had never lost control over his estates. The attempt of the Commissioners for Forfeited Estates to take them over foundered on their physical remoteness (being north-west of Inverness); the loyalty of his clansmen; and the aggressive tactics of his devoted factor who not only collected the rents for despatch to Seaforth abroad, but also hired bands of cutthroats with whom he successfully put the fear of death into the odd government official foolish enough to stray into Mackenzie territory. Participation in the '19 seems to have cured Seaforth of any enthusiasm for the Jacobite cause. He remained faithful to the deal he cut with the Hanoverians, and though he lost his title, his grandson was allowed to purchase an impeccable legal succession to the estates and given the title of Viscount Fortrose in the Irish peerage. By 1771 the Seaforth earldom had been recreated for the family.

Jacobitism did, however, survive in Scotland, despite the carrot and stick methods whereby Whig governments tried to eradicate it. For Seaforth in 1726 the carrot of restored property was held out. In 1717 Royal Commissioners had taken a stick to the notoriously Jacobite twin universities at Aberdeen — King's College, and Marischal College. Ten professors were purged, six at Marischal, and four at King's, including Principal George Middleton. As was the case with deposed Episcopal clergy, the result of such purges tended to be a spreading of embittered educated Jacobites through the North-East. In St Andrews a Commission of Visitation in 1718 worked much less drastically. They did manage to suspend a blatant case of disaffection in the shape of Alexander Scrimgeour (in Jacobite eyes the rightful fourth Earl of Dundee), a Jacobite Episcopalian layman who, quite bizarrely, managed to secure appointment as Professor of Ecclesiastical History in 1713. Though suspended from teaching, he died still in full possession of his chair's emoluments in 1732. The real difficulty for the Whigs was the way in which Jacobite views were embedded in the Scottish aristocracy. Most Fife lairds, for example, remained tainted with Jacobite policies and Episcopal religion and their views were bound to affect the atmosphere of the University of St Andrews. A good example is the family of the Scots of Scotstarvit whose most illustrious head, Sir John Scot of Scotstarvit, had been a notable early seventeenth-century benefactor of the university. He lived in an austere tower-house which still rears its noble shape on a hill above Cupar. His eighteenth-century descendents, like many Scots lairds, abandoned its functional austerity for a Georgian mansion, Hill of Tarvit, just across the road. After a notable early twentieth-century renovation for a Dundee jute millionaire, the mansion, with his art collection, is now cared for by the National Trust for Scotland. What mattered in the first half of the eighteenth century was that the Scots of Scotstarvit were Jacobites and patrons of the Chair of Humanity (or Latin) in St Andrews.

Wherever a community of Scottish lairds was deeply disgruntled about a local Whig ascendancy, there Jacobitism was liable to flourish. An unlikely example is Orkney, where the Douglas Earls of Morton, after a very chequered career in Orkney and Shetland, emerged as virtual rulers of both island groups between 1707 and 1766. The Earls of Morton adopted an ultra-royalist line for much of the seventeenth century, but they then jumped on the bandwagon of the 1688 Revolution and showed subservience to government wishes during the negotiations for the Act of Union. As a reward, the Crown gave them possession of the earldom of Orkney estates, subject to a right of redemption. To these properties they subsequently added the tack or lease of the lapsed bishopric estates, which gave them most of the rest of the Northern Isles. In the dying days of the administration of Sir Robert Walpole the fourteenth Earl of Morton obtained the absolute lordship of Orkney and Shetland when the Crown abandoned its right of redemption. The Morton earls also held Admiralty jurisdiction, lucrative because of the frequency of wrecks. The Morton regime was profoundly unpopular with the Orkney lairds, who fought it over its demands for feudal dues and over local ecclesiastical and political patronage. It is hardly surprising that the most vocal opponent of the Earl of Morton, Sir James Steuart of Burray, emerged as head of a faction of active Jacobite sympathisers among the Orkney lairds. When local power so obviously depended on favour with central government, the discontented looked for a change of government, and if they were convinced Jacobites they thought in terms of a Stuart restoration.

Discontent was rife in Britain in the period 1720-1744. The government was based on a virtual putsch by the Whigs in the aftermath of the Hanoverian succession. The Tory party survived, banned from office and with a significant Jacobite minority in it. Whig power was buttressed by a battery of legislation designed to strengthen an unpopular executive representing only minority opinion. The '15 provided a wonderful excuse for legislation such as the Riot Act, designed to limit popular protest; and the Septennial Act, which abolished the existing system of three-yearly elections and substituted the vast period of seven years, avowedly to render MPs virtually immune to pressure from disgruntled constituents. When bodies like the Common Council of the City of London challenged the wishes of the Whig Prime Minister, Sir Robert Walpole, he promptly introduced legislation to restrict its powers and to increase those of a City oligarchy of very rich merchants amenable to manipulation by government. The representative body of the Church of England was suspended indefinitely because of the intransigent Toryism of the bulk of the lower clergy. Wherever possible municipal franchises were restricted to reinforce Whig ascendancy. Glasgow's resistance to government in 1725 had been crushed by Wade and the Lord Advocate of Scotland, Duncan Forbes of Culloden, a Highland laird who was principal man of business to the Duke of Argyll. When in 1736 Edinburgh burst into riotous protest against the unpopular Customs and Excise system and lynched the brutal commander of the city guard, Captain Porteous, Walpole responded with fierce communal punishment designed to daunt the city and degrade its rulers (most of whom had clearly had no hand in the riot). Both Wade and Argyll opposed the legislation as harsh and counter-productive. Simon Fraser Lord Lovat, Scottish patriot as well as crypto-Jacobite, considered the punitive legislation following the Porteous affair as the supreme proof of Scotland's degradation. So far from serving as a palladium of liberties, the Westminster legislature was showing only too often the ugly face of a club of largely irresponsible politicians, hostile to all liberty except their own.

The key to all of this was the emergence of Sir Robert Walpole as the dominant political boss of his generation. His ascendancy was born in corruption, for he gained power in the aftermath of the South Sea Bubble scandal of 1721, an episode in which key members of the government actively promoted a massive stock swindle. Walpole served his masters well by sacrificing only those politicians who could not be saved, and by resisting pressure for an enquiry which would probably have revealed that the Hanoverian royal family itself was involved in malpractice. Like all English politicians, Sir Robert would have preferred not to have a local political manager for Scotland (since such a manager necessarily acquired a measure of bargaining power) but in the end he ran Scotland through a Campbell political machine headed by John Duke of Argyll and Greenwich, the hero of Sheriffmuir, and his infinitely slippery brother the Earl of Ilay, who succeeded as third Duke of Argyll, but who is usually known as Ilay. Walpole had not, like a twentieth-century Prime Minister, actually replaced the nominal sovereign as effective monarch, and he had to deal with a House of Lords with an independent hereditary majority rather than a chamber nominated by the Prime Minister, as was to be the case in the latter part of the twentieth century; nevertheless in many ways he anticipated the elective dictatorship of his modern successors. With solid support from George I and George II he did have monarchical power at his disposal. Bishops and placemen normally gave him the initiative in the Lords, and an elaborate structure of patronage normally enabled him to swing enough additional support behind his placemen in the Commons to secure victory.

Like many Prime Ministers, he was passionately jealous of men of ability who might become potential rivals. The Campbell brothers were too strong to be ignored in Scotland, but Ilay understood well that he must not raise policy issues. His authority in Scotland was strictly a mechanism for channelling places and pensions into the hands of the Argylls. Anyone not a follower of Argyll tended to have a thin time of it, and it was a matter of anguish to Simon Fraser Lord Lovat that, despite endless sycophancy on his part, Ilay would not take him aboard the Argathelian ship for the purpose of sharing in its regular rations of loaves and fishes to the crew. Sheer bad luck could lead to frustration and disappointment for major Highland magnates in so narrowly-based a spoils system.

A good example of the phenomenon was young Ludovick Grant of Grant, chief of his clan, a trained lawyer, and lord of a great regality on Speyside. It had been created for his family as compensation for Jacobite attacks on their estates at the time of the Glorious Revolution, of which they had been staunch supporters. They had been equally active Whigs in 1715-16, at great expense, none of which Westminster saw fit to repay. Ludovick Grant was an MP at one point, but the height of his ambition was to gain a place on the Court of Session, Scotland's highest civil court. Unfortunately, he had crossed the Argyll faction at the start of his political career, and no amount of subsequent grovelling would make Ilay disgorge a judge-ship for Ludovick Grant. By the early 1740s Ludovick had retired to his estates to live frugally in an effort to restore his fortune. It was no accident that he refused to take expensive action on behalf of the government in 1745-46, and that the two outlying parts of the Grant clan lands — Glen Urquhart and Glenmoriston — went Jacobite.

The Whig politicians in office had assumed all the airs and arro-gance of the 'Court' style of politics originally associated with the later Stuarts. All Tories became exponents of the anti-executive 'Country' style, as indeed did a substantial body of Whigs who did not hold office. Nearly all British Jacobites adopted 'Country' atti-tudes which meant that in practice they accused the Whig regime of betraying precisely those values which the Glorious Revolution was supposed to have preserved. Certainly words like 'representation', 'responsibility', and 'liberty', sat ill on regimes which claimed abso-lute unbridled power for their partially-tame legislature, and which worked relentlessly to minimise the ability of voters to influence MPs. The argument that MPs, once elected, must be free to use their judgement was humbug on the lips of men dedicated to bullying and persuading MPs with threats and offers of pensions and places. The one Achilles' heel of the system was the existence in the Commons of a solid block of English backbenchers who were independent of government patronage. Scots MPs tended to be subservient, but the independent English country gentlemen ensured that the legisla-ture was not as puny in the face of the executive as it was to become in the days of modern mass party machines. The independents were conservative men, but they could combine with disgruntled opposi-tion politicians to overthrow a government, in exceptional cases, as indeed they did when Walpole fell in 1742. Ironically, it then became clear that the leading Westminster critics of Walpole's system did not really object to the system, but to the fact that they were not cut into it. Walpole's successor and pupil Henry Pelham adopted a pol-icy of incorporating opposition leaders and was eventually able to reconstruct Walpole's system. Opinion out of doors was deeply, and rightly, disillusioned.

It is nevertheless a fatal error to assume that the word 'Country' is the same as the word 'Jacobite' in eighteenth-century politics. Most Jacobites were 'Country' in views, but most 'Country' opinion, including most Tory opinion, was emphatically not 'Jacobite'. Dr Johnson's much later remark that most Britons would vote for the Pretender is nostalgic nonsense from the mouth of an arch-reac-tionary (and pensioner of George III). There was a minority of Jacobites, just as there was a minority of Whigs, and there was a majority of apathetic or disgruntled Britons. Had Britain not been drifting into war with France, this would scarcely have mattered, but she was.

War was the one stress which could threaten Walpole's system, as he well knew, which is why he was only very reluctantly hounded into declaring war on the Bourbon monarchy of Spain in 1739, over the old issue of British access to areas of Spanish ascendancy in the Americas. In 1740 central Europe was convulsed by the outbreak of the War of the Austrian Succession and in France the cautious octogenarian Cardinal Fleury was pushed aside by a war party led by Marshal Belle-Isle who wanted to join in the offensive against Britain's traditional ally, Austria. Even under Fleury, France would not have allowed Britain to dismantle the Spanish empire. Nor was Britain even likely to stand by while France demolished Austria. By 1743 a full-scale Anglo-French war was in progress, though neither power had declared war on the other. They preserved the fiction that they appeared on battlefields merely as auxiliaries. After George II had led the 'Pragmatic Army' of German mercenaries to a surprise victory over the French at Dettingen, in June 1743, something like a stalemate emerged. George's principal English minister, Carteret, suffered from delusions about repeating the triumphs of Marlborough over Louis XIV, and the France of Louis XV began to search for ways of forcing an end to an expensive war.

One obvious answer was a successful invasion of England on behalf of the exiled Stuarts. For a long time the French had been quite pleased with the presence of the Elector of Hanover on the British thrones, because it deprived Britain of the advantages of being an island. Any overseas losses to British naval power could usually be recouped by sending a French army to occupy Hanover. Carteret's 'meddle and muddle' policy in Europe had by 1744 ensured a change of heart in French government circles. After the death of Cardinal Fleury at the age of 90 in January 1743, Louis XV appointed no principal minister, which, given his own aversion to business, meant that France was really ruled by her four secretaries of state. They began to feel that, as their partnership with the House of Hanover had crumbled since the late 1730s, there was a case for a Stuart restoration; this would continue the trade relations which France had profitably enjoyed with Britain since 1713, but would also put an end to continual meddling in Continental affairs by British governments. Francis, Lord Semphill, the exiled and disinherited son of a Scots peer who was the Pretender's representative at the French court, soon conveyed the exciting news to his master that France was talking about an invasion of England, and that for once the French seemed to mean what they said. Serious preparations for invasion began in November 1743. After a second Jacobite agent, William MacGregor (or Drummond) of Balhaldy, had prepared the way, the Pretender's eldest son Prince Charles Edward Stuart journeyed to Paris late in January 1744 to act as nominal commander of the invasion force.

Charles had no real military experience apart from having shown his face at an Italian siege. The real commander was to be the first Marshal of France, Maurice Comte de Saxe, one of the innumerable bastards of Augustus the Strong of Poland-Saxony. The French would have no truck with a diversionary attack in Scotland. The idea was to land 10,000 troops near London, fight and win a decisive battle, and then rely on political realities to secure a Stuart regime. The combination of an active Jacobite element; demoralised and unpopular Whigs; and widespread English apathy allied to instinctive deference to centralised rule, was thought to be enough if de Saxe could first win his fight. Politically, the French were shrewd. They made no territorial demands on Britain. As soon as the decisive battle had been won, de Saxe was to be replaced as military commander by the old Tory hero Ormonde. The new regime was pledged to the repeal of the Septennial Act and to the passing of an act against placemen in the legislature. Such a British regime would probably have had difficulty pursuing any interventionist foreign policy in Europe, which of course suited France, but given Carteret's record of non-achievement, it was possible to argue that this would be good for Europe. A future Stuart sovereign would be able to mobilise men and money to defend any clearly perceived British interest which was threatened, provided public opinion was behind him.

There were snags in the conception of the invasion. Maurice de Saxe was against it from the start because the naval side was risky, and defeat in the land battle meant total eclipse. He was supposed to take his troopships from Dunkirk to the Thames estuary, piloted by two professional smugglers Thomas Harvey and Robert Fuller. In fact he would have preferred to disembark them for an invasion of Austrian Flanders. In any case security was blown by a French spy in British pay, and Admiral Norris was soon in a position to block any invasion. The King of France had been rather keen on invading a country with which he was not even technically at war, but by the time war was declared in March 1744, France had postponed the idea indefinitely. Maurice de Saxe set off on his invasion of Flanders.

In a sense, the abortive '44 is itself a sufficient explanation for the '45. Prince Charles was only 24 in '44 but he knew that if France lost interest in his dynasty, it was the end of all his hopes. He hung around in the dreary seaside town of Gravelines until the spring, but by the summer he was in Paris. His debts grew, as did his distrust of Semphill, Balhaldy, and Louis XV. By late 1744 and early 1745 he was skulking in country houses in northern France talking long and hard to exiled Jacobites and French sympathisers. What they said was true: the only way to force the government of Louis XV to reverse its policy was to go to Britain and start a rebellion so successful that France could not afford not to intervene. Time was short, for peace might break out at any moment. The Earl of Morton had crossed to France, ostensibly on private business, but in reality to try to negotiate a peace settlement on behalf of the British ministry. He was to be in France much longer that he expected, for he was overtaken by the outbreak of the '45 rebellion in Scotland and latterly held as a hostage for the safety of captured Jacobite rebels.

The obvious place for the Jacobite Prince of Wales to land was in the Highlands of Scotland. There had been an Association of Jacobite leaders meeting informally in Scotland since rumours of war started to fly in 1738. They were hardly 'the origin of the '45' since only three of them — the Duke of Perth, Lovat, and Lochiel — came out in the '45, but they did help keep contacts with the exiled court very active. Over and over again, they said another rebellion would only be justified if France committed significant numbers of troops, large sums of money, and many weapons. The principal contact between the Associators and Prince Charles was John Murray of Broughton, who was to be secretary to Charles in 1745-46. In 1743-44 he shuttled between Scotland and France always hearing the same, sensible, view in Scotland that without about 6,000 French regulars, arms for 10,000 more and 30,000 louis d'or, rebellion would be suicide. Meantime Prince Charles had established contact with French Jacobite privateers of Irish extraction who stood only to gain from a rebellion which would divert Royal Navy units away from convoy duty.

It was these men, D'Heguerty, Walter Ruttledge of Dunkirk, Butler of St Malo, and above all Antoine Walsh of Nantes, slaver, privateer and, as he himself always stressed, patriotic Frenchman, who launched the '45 with a hired French battleship *L'Elisabeth* (a 64-gun British prize), and what Walsh called 'a little frigate, a good sailor' called *Le du Teillay.* The Prince, his small entourage and Walsh sailed from the Loire in the latter, while the former joined them from Brest. Aboard were 40,000 livres worth of weapons: muskets, broadswords, and twenty small field pieces, as well as ammunition. The Prince had run into debt to buy them, but he also carried a cash reserve of 4,000 louis d'or. Procedures did exist which should have enabled the French Ministry of Marine to know what was being done with a warship they were leasing out. The assembling of the arms and ammunition had been expressly authorised by the Ministry of War, and if Jacobite funds paid for the company of French volunteer officers and cadets aboard *L'Elisabeth,* they were still uniformed regulars. With so many accomplished liars, and so few who wanted to know what was really going on, it is difficult to apportion responsibility.

A few days out on a course to round Ireland on the way to the Outer Hebrides, Charles was given a lesson in naval power when HMS *Lyon,* a newly-refitted 58-gun ship, caught his squadron off the Lizard. *L'Elisabeth* sacrificed herself in a vicious day-long duel which left both big ships bloody and so battered they had to return to port. Walsh crowded on sail for the Hebrides, the expedition now reduced to Prince Charles and his dozen or so companions, of whom, despite much romantic talk of 'the seven men of Moidart', one of the most useful was probably a servant of Lochiel, Duncan Cameron, a native of Barra who could act as pilot in the Hebrides. On 23 July 1745 the Hebrides were sighted. Anchoring off Barra, Charles sent Aeneas MacDonald, a Parisian banker in his suite, ashore to contact his brother-in-law Roderick MacNeil of Barra He came back in a panic. The MacNeil was away from home, and there was news that the government had just arrested Sir Hector MacLean of Duart, the leading Jacobite chief in Mull. At this point Sir Thomas Sheridan, an old Irish veteran of the Battle of the Boyne, and the Duke of Atholl were for going back. Walsh and Prince Charles were for going on.

Events forced *Le du Teillay* into an anchorage between Barra and South Uist, where on the rocky islet of Eriskay MacDonald of Clanranald's brother, Alexander MacDonald of Boisdale, met with the Prince and his men. Boisdale told them to go home. Not only would he not join them in an irresponsible gamble, but he brought news that the two key chiefs in the Isle of Skye, Sir Alexander MacDonald of Sleat and Norman MacLeod of MacLeod, did not propose to honour their pledges to join Charles. They had a point, for they had told him repeatedly he must come with French men, weapons and money. Coming unsupported was virtually a confidence trick. He had nothing to lose; they everything. Much more disreputable was

14. *Glenfinnan, where Prince Charles raised his standard at the start of the '45. The 1820 monument is now in the care of the National Trust for Scotland*

15. *Culloden, where the National Trust for Scotland has recently
    cleared forestry, thus revealing the clear field of fire
    for the Hanoverian artillery in 1746*

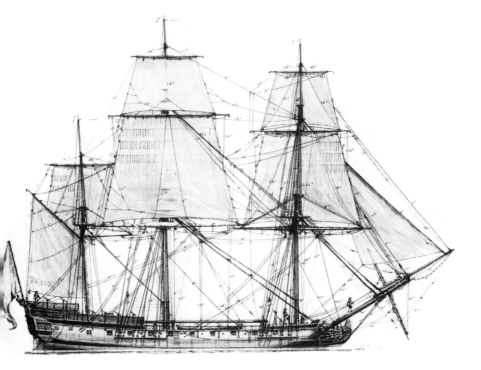

Le du Teillay, *a reconstruction of the ship which brought
Prince Charles to Scotland to start the '45*

the blackmail held over their heads by the Whig judge Duncan
Forbes of Culloden, that if they stepped out of line he might prose-
cute them for the early clearances they had allegedly been perpe-
trating by kidnapping surplus tenants for sale as bond servants
(virtual slaves) in America.

Charles then showed the incredible willpower without which
there would have been no '45. He decided to sail for the mainland,
anchoring at Loch nan Uamh, a sea loch between Arisaig and Moidart. Almost at once Aeneas MacDonald brought his brother Mac-
Donald of Kinlochmoidart and Clanranald to meet him. For ten
days he stayed aboard ship arguing with a succession of Jacobite
visitors, all loyally willing to support a rising in force but appalled by
his unsupported arrival. The region of Arisaig was a safe one for the
Prince. It was almost entirely Catholic and he was unlikely to be har-
rassed by Whig opponents, but the real struggle was for the minds of

Scotsmen — and for that of Louis XV. On 6 August Charles wrote to Louis announcing his arrival in Scotland, and appealing for aid which, he said, would enable him to invade England. James the Old Pretender also wrote to Louis saying, truthfully, that he was as surprised as anyone at the news of his son's venture and that he had for some time wanted to surrender all his claims to Charles. Charles reached Scotland as Jacobite Prince Regent. Had he entered London, James would probably have abdicated at once to let his son reign as Charles III.

Our knowledge of his debates aboard the ship is hazy. Charles is said to have moved many MacDonald chiefs by an appeal to Kinlochmoidart's brother Ranald, who swore to die for him, if need be alone. Chiefs like MacDonell of Keppoch and Alasdair MacDonald of Glencoe were fairly predictable backers of any rising, but simply not important enought to lift one off the ground. For that Charles needed the biggest man in Lochaber — Donald Cameron Younger of Lochiel, an Episcopalian gentleman of considerable enterprise. The chiefs of Clan Cameron had been speculating in American land for at least a generation. They sold timber for charcoal for ironworks, and they spent much time in Edinburgh. Donald's father was still in exile in France after his role in the '15. Financially Lochaber was in dire straits. Bad harvests after 1741 had plunged Scotland to the brink of famine. It did not come but the '45 was played out in a half-starved Highlands where rents were in arrears and cattle difficult to sell. Lochiel, known to history as 'the gentle Lochiel' of the '45, was on the verge of ruin, many of his debts being in the hands of his devious brother John of Fassifern, a very successful man of business, who tried to talk Lochiel out of meeting Charles. He may well have been primarily interested in the family property, on which he might soon be foreclosing, but he is said to have warned Lochiel that Charles would sweep him off his feet. He hardly did that. Charles seems to have advanced two arguments, both convincing, as well as making the emotional appeal which could not but stir a Jacobite heart. The first argument was that Scotland was so scandalously badly defended that a quick seizure of power would be easy. The second was that he could guarantee Lochiel more than his present income even if the rebellion failed. Here Charles did keep his word, by securing for Lochiel after 1746 a French regiment worth more than his estates. The die was cast when Charles sent Walsh back to France. A rebellion was now the only option left.

The Jacobite standard was raised on Monday, 19 August 1745 in Glenfinnan, in Clanranald's country near the Cameron lands. At the

head of Loch Shiel, where three glens open out, it was both accessible and remote and defensible. Clanranald was by now committed.
MacDonald of Morar arrived with 150 men. After two hours of
suspense Lochiel came in with 600 or 700. MacDonell of Keppoch,
prince of Highland bandits, came in with 300 of his fierce little clan,
not to mention nearly 70 men of the Royal Scots who had been captured after being ambushed eight miles north of Fort William by an
inferior force of Keppoch's people. With 1,100-1,500 men, the rebellion was clearly a going concern, especially as it was known that
chiefs like Stewart of Appin were raising their people. Atholl acted
as standard-bearer as the Roman Catholic Bishop Hugh Mac-
Donald blessed it. Privately the good bishop thought the whole
episode a sorry business, but he could not stop his people. King
James was proclaimed. The commission to Charles as Prince Regent
was read. Finally the Jacobite leaders were reminded that they were
committed to political acts as well as a person when the clansmen
cheered and shouted 'Long live King James VIII and Charles Prince
of Wales; prosperity to Scotland and no Union!'

The arms brought from *Le du Teillay* were first stored in Castle
Tioram on Loch Moidart, then distributed to the troops. They came
in the form of a 'stand' of arms i.e. a musket, bayonet, and brass-
hilted hanger or infantryman's sword. The Highlanders had little
time for hanger or bayonet, much preferring their own basket-hilted
broadswords, but they liked the muskets. Charles also had two
dozen light swivel guns of one or two pound calibre. They had light
field carriages, but horses were very scarce in the Jacobite camp and
the guns were abandoned at an early stage in the campaign. The
army began to march west almost at once, picking up recruits and,
one tradition says, its campaign badge of the white rose from bushes
at Fassifern. Everyone expected a general action soon, a 'battle in
Badenoch'. The Hanoverian commander in Scotland, General Sir
John Cope, was expected to come north and fight, if only to spare the
Lowlands from a descent by hordes of clansmen desperate after
several hard winters.

Cope intended to do just that, despite the low number and poor
quality of his troops — a mere 4,000 in all excluding the 'invalid' garrisons of Stirling, Dumbarton, and Edinburgh Castles, composed of
men unfit for field service. Of his 4,000, only a small proportion were
veteran. He had three and a half line regiments, of which only one
pre-dated 1741 or had seen any action. Nine companies of raw recruits raised as reinforcements to be drafted to serving regiments
were nearly as useless as the half-raised Highland regiment which

*Edinburgh Castle, which never fell to the Jacobites
in the course of the '45 (from an engraving by Paul Sandby)*

the Campbell Lord Loudon was trying to pull together as the rebellion started. For cavalry he had two weak regiments of Irish dragoons with young troop horses not yet trained to the noise of firearms. If there were plenty of artillery pieces lying around the castles, there was not one trained gunner in Scotland. It was not so much an army as a basic training camp. Yet Prince Charles's venture, now known to have no visible French backing, hardly sounded like a serious rebellion. Cope tried to deal with it as Wightman with the '19. He concentrated his forces and marched north, lugging many additional stands of arms on the assumption that thousands of loyal Whig Highlanders would flock to him to repair his weaknesses in light troops. His first shock was their failure to appear, underlined by Whig magnates like the Earl of Breadalbane and the Duke of Atholl who told him just how little positive love there was for the Westminster government even in their lands.

Charles and his men faced no serious problem with the Highland forts. They moved rapidly past them to seize the Pass of Corrieyair-rack, the key to a rapid break-out, and also the objective of Cope's march, though he was thinking of moving into the Great Glen to link up with the garrison of Fort Augustus. Storming the zigzags lined with Jacobite musketeers would have been a guaranteed fiasco and a bloody one, so an unnerved Cope marched rapidly for Inverness, whence he eventually moved to Aberdeen prior to shipping his army back to the Edinburgh region. The upshot was that, to their amazement, the Jacobites found that they faced no opposition at all in the course of their march south. Charles and several thousand friends just walked to Edinburgh. That is a slight over-simplification, for there were still two Hanoverian regiments ahead of them under the command of the 85-year-old General Joshua Guest. Still, by 4 September the Jacobite army was in Perth, where it recruited for a week.

Here Charles acquired his two Lieutenant-Generals, Lord George Murray, born in 1694 and a younger brother of the Duke of Atholl. A British regular officer who had turned Jacobite at the time of the '15, he had been 'out' in the '19 and was lucky to be given a pardon, after which he had lived very quietly in Perthshire. His decision to join Charles was a hard one. Nobody was going to argue that he should be pardoned again if the rising failed, and he appears to have taken his decision out of a sense of duty and leaning heavily on two assurances with which Charles was very free. One was that the French were absolutely committed to send massive assistance soon. The other was that he was in contact with many English Jacobites only waiting for the signal to rise. Neither statement was true.

Lord George was the military genius of the '45, a very great master of light infantry warfare, and a gallant, sensible gentleman, if hot-tempered. Fortunately the other Lieutenant-General, the Roman Catholic James Drummond, Jacobite Duke of Perth, a 34-year-old gentleman educated in France, proved an admirable foil. Perth was gentle, modest, and universally esteemed. They had to try to create together an army out of a mass of Highland peasants, reinforced by the usual strong Lowland contingent from the Jacobite and Episcopal North-East of Banffshire and Aberdeenshire, but with precious few other Lowlanders, in part because of the total hostility of the Presbyterian Kirk. At least they found Guest's men little problem. All they faced were the two feeble dragoon regiments commanded by Colonel Gardiner, once a fire-eater, but now, though still brave, a mental and physical wreck. They made no attempt to contest the crossing of the Forth and even so brisk a com-

Lord George Murray, the best Jacobite general of the '45,
in his campaign dress

mander as Lord George Murray could not catch them as they with-
drew past Edinburgh, to link up with Cope who was finally shipping
his men to Dunbar, the most accessible good harbour east of the
capital.

The 'fall' of Edinburgh was pure comic opera. Local Whigs

formed a Volunteer Corps to defend the city, but when assembled, it became clear that few of the privates wished to march to reinforce the dragoons. The latter were then seen conducting a rapid tactical retreat on the other side of the Nor Loch (along the future line of Princes Street), and the venerable Dr William Wishart who was Principal of Edinburgh University argued passionately that amateur resistance would simply lead to a massacre 'without any just or adequate object'. Provost Stuart was clearly of the same mind. The Westminster government was not worth dying for, the more so as it was doing its best to crush what little self-government was left to the burgh of Edinburgh through its local hatchet man the arch-Whig George Drummond. Charles's men rushed an open city gate and occupied the town. After the rebellion Provost Stuart was tried for Jacobitism, but as he could be convicted only of common-sense, the charge failed.

Holding court at Holyrood, Charles continued to recruit. Among others, he was joined at Edinburgh by Lord Elcho who was to command his Life Guard. Politically, the Whigs were in confusion. The bulk of the population showed no love for them, if little positive Jacobitism. The greatest Whig clan, the Campbells, had been fatally weakened by the second Duke of Argyll's policy of squeezing out Campbell tacksmen, the officers of the clan army, in order to maximise his own rents. Ilay succeeded to the dukedom in 1743 and tried to reverse the policy, too late. Besides, the political confusion following the fall of Walpole had riven what Scottish administration there was with feud and faction. Secretary for Scotland Lord Tweeddale and his political appointments were locked in feud with Argyll, who was supported by the judges, most of whom owed their jobs to him. Duncan Forbes, as Lord President of the Court of Session, was rather detached from politics, but he was an Argyll man, while Andrew Fletcher, Lord Milton, Lord Justice Clerk from 1735 to 1748, was Argyll's *alter ego* in North Britain. The sole Whig hope lay in the fact that Charles still had only 2,500 men, and Cope had at last arrived.

Disembarking at Dunbar, Cope adopted a good defensive line with one flank on the sea at Prestonpans and his front protected by the bog known as 'Tranent Meadows'. In numbers the two armies were equal. Local guides took the Jacobite army through the marsh in the half-light of early morning and enabled them partially to outflank Cope, who had to swing round and fight with his back to Edinburgh. The initiative was siezed by Lord George who launched his infantry into the attack in two masses. Firing as they came, they closed with the broadsword. Cope's untrained gunners fled. Colonel Gardiner sacrificed his life in vain setting an example to his dragoons, for they broke, and the government infantry panicked *en masse*. It was all over in quarter of an hour. Discipline alone enabled regular troops to withstand mass attack. Musket fire was only effective at a range of under a hundred yards, and even then only as massed volleys, because of the innacuracy of individual weapons. Firing case shot, field guns could be used to check the last stages of an assault by discharging containers loaded with bullets which sprayed out from the muzzle. This form of projectile is often loosely called grape shot, though grape was properly a very heavy version of case shot with too few projectiles for efficient land use. It was primarily naval. However, case could only be used by trained gunners with nerve to wait to the last minute.

Charles was master of Scotland. Cope fled for Berwick, and recruitment to the Jacobite army accelerated. It still represented only a tiny minority. Inverness was in Whig hands and Lord President Forbes and Lord Loudon were raising Whig independent companies in the Highlands to enable them to control most territory north of Inverness. Seaforth refused to rise. It was his rival for the Mackenzie leadership, Lord Cromartie, who mobilised some Mackenzies for Charles. No great magnate committed himself. The Whig Duke of Atholl remained aloof, though Lord George Murray and the Jacobite Duke William raised an Atholl Brigade for Charles. The Duke of Gordon stayed aloof. Charles could compensate partially through the help of Lord Lewis Gordon, a junior member of the ducal family, just as he could outflank the Whiggery of Mackintosh of Mackintosh by the fierce Jacobitism of his wife. The rather undersexed Charles appealed to the ladies.

In his council at Holyrood a furious debate raged. There was no agreement on future strategy. The great Scottish castles were still unconquered. In October three French ships reached Montrose and Stonehaven, with some regular troops, a few light guns and gunners, and an emissary, the Marquis d'Eguilles, who had come to fish in troubled waters. He brought no clear commitment. Most of the Scottish Jacobites would have preferred to try to consolidate in Scotland, hoping that even France would eventually send help, simply because an independent Scotland would suit her well. Charles thought of nothing but England, and the clique of Irish advisers on whom he increasingly leaned naturally shared his views. By a majority of one vote it was decided to invade England. On 3 November 1745 a force of 5,000 foot and 500 horse crossed the Border in the

*The Whig Duncan Forbes of Culloden, wearing the civil robes of
the Lord President of the Court of Session*

face of three Whig Army groups reinforced by Dutch troops and
men recalled from Flanders.

Though Charles put all his men in Highland dress, his army was
no horde of 'bare-arsed banditti', to use a contemporary Whig term
of abuse. Charles had been given a complete set of Highland dress
by 'his' Duke of Perth in 1740. His younger brother Henry was also

A Highland targe. Prince Charles's infantry carried one

given the same present. Part of it may survive in the wonderful sil-
ver-mounted 'Prince's Targe' and a broadsword, both of which
eventually came into the collections of the National Museum of
Antiquities. About the same period 1740-41 Charles was also given
the beautiful rococo canteen of silver-gilt travelling cutlery made by
an Edinburgh craftsman from the ultra-Jacobite Oliphant of Gask
family. Highland dress and rococo canteen went on campaign in
1745-46, but as part of an orthodox eighteenth-century army organised in a Highland and a Lowland Division. The units were regi-
mented and only the biggest clans had their own regiments. Others
were grouped. The colonels were a mixed bag. Macpherson of
Cluny was virtually kidnapped into the rebellion by Lochiel, but two
better regimental commanders would be difficult to imagine than
Cluny and Lochiel in the '45. Many Jacobite officers, like Lord
George Murray, had held commissions in the French or British
armies and the rare surviving regimental order books show a very
orthodox pattern of administration. Discipline was humane and
effective. English deference to authority enabled the Jacobites to

collect local revenues as they advanced, and eliminated any need for plundering.

The advance was incredibly lucky. Charles had no artillery capable of serious siege-work, yet the once important fortress of Carlisle rapidly and disgracefully surrendered to little more than a blockade. Wade was at Newcastle with an army including the Dutch troops, but he misjudged the Jacobite invasion route and then his advanced age and severe snowy weather prevented him from crossing the Pennines to engage his foe. A much better general, the French Huguenot General Sir John Ligonier, commanded in the Midlands, but after the Jacobites raced down Lancashire to occupy Manchester, he was outmanoeuvred and shocked to find the enemy at Derby, within striking distance of London. By then it was clear that the Jacobites had just enough horse for vital patrol and scouting work, but their luck was running out.

The English Establishment, having botched the defence of Scotland, bade fair to do the same with England. Obsessed with their role as Good Europeans, they refused to take the rebellion seriously, dragging their feet over withdrawing men from Flanders, the focus of European power-politics. However, the Duke of Cumberland, soldier son of George II, had eventually come over with much of his Flanders command to replace Ligonier. The Guards shielded London on the north. An army guarded the south coast against invasion. At Derby the Jacobites argued in council.

Even at Carlisle Lord George Murray and the chiefs had challenged the truth of the letters from English Jacobites which Charles said he had. The lack of any rising by English Tories deeply depressed the Scots. A Manchester Regiment was the only significant English Jacobite unit, and it owed its existence to Roman Catholics and the local unemployed. By Derby Charles had to admit he was not even in contact with the English Tories. Then there was the matter of the French. Of course the success of the rising made them re-activate invasion plans and wheel in Prince Henry Stuart as the nominal leader, but it was all far too late and it was clear that Charles had again lied when he said the French were committed before he came. Indeed they were not. He came to try to commit them. Put in these terms there was only one likely decision at Derby — retreat. Charles was beside himself with chagrin, but even heroes do not put themselves in a suicidal position for someone who has just conned them. Had they raced forward, they might have smashed the Guards, but they were in a position where defeat meant obliteration. Lord George's conduct of the long retreat was in

Stirling Castle, besieged unsuccessfully by Prince Charles's army during the '45 (from an engraving by Paul Sandby)

fact inspired and his neutralisation of Cumberland's superior cavalry remarkable. South of Carlisle the Jacobites turned and savaged Cumberland's advanced guard at Penrith. On 20 December 1745, Charles's 25th birthday, his army crossed the Esk back into Scotland.

The situation in Scotland was complex enough. The Jacobite power-base was very narrow. Whereas in the '15 the Jacobites had held elections in east-coast burghs, assured of a favourable result, Charles had to appoint regional governors. Cope's successor, General Handasyde, had marched up from Berwick and occupied Edinburgh when Charles left for England. Loudon and Forbes held the north for Hanover. In Argyll General Sir John Campbell of Mamore was licking a Campbell militia into shape. At Perth the Jacobite Lord Strathallan had built up a second army of 3-4,000 men. It included Lord John Drummond who had come from France with elements of his own regiment, and of the Irish Brigade in French service. He also brought a few heavy guns with him and with these Prince Charles set about besieging Stirling Castle after screwing a heavy tribute for the maintenance of his army out of reluctant Whig Glasgow.

Under an incompetent Franco-Scot, aptly named Mirabel de Gordon, the siege made absolutely no progress. Meantime the garrison Charles had wilfully insisted on leaving in Carlisle had fallen into the clutches of Cumberland, due to ominously good artillery work by Cumberland's leading gunner, Major William Belford. Lieutenant-General Henry Hawley, the brutal and clumsy new Hanoverian commander in Edinburgh, still had no trained artillerists, apart from an eighteen-year-old boy. Hawley also suffered from the illusion that Highlanders would run from a cavalry charge. When Hawley blundered forward to relieve Stirling, Lord George Murray snatched a spectacular victory on 17 January 1746 in an encounter battle at Falkirk, fought in foul weather. Highland musketry stopped Hawley's cavalry, and a downhill charge swept away half his infantry. It was a bad omen that Price's, Ligonier's, and Barrel's Regiments stood firm.

With Cumberland in command of veteran troops, and Belford in charge of his excellent field artillery, the days of easy victories were over. Charles retreated to Crieff where his army split into two divisions, one of which marched through the Grampians to Inverness and the other under Lord George went there by coast road. They met at Inverness two days after Loudon evacuated the town. Fort George fell quickly, and Fort Augustus surrendered after a lucky mortar shot blew up its magazine, but Fort William, commanded by the ruthless Captain Caroline Scott, proved too tough a nut, despite the anxiety of the Camerons and MacDonalds to take it. Under the absurd Mirabel, the Jacobite besiegers made no progress. In a brilliant little campaign north of Inverness, which owed not a little to Jacobite animus against the three Whig leaders there — Forbes of Culloden, MacLeod of MacLeod, and Loudon — the Whig Highland levies were routed and chased literally off the mainland to Skye. The real menace to Charles was, however, the advance of Cumberland.

By March Cumberland was in Aberdeen. Inverness was the last town capable of being a Jacobite base. A final Jacobite sally against Whig militia posts in the Tay Valley was sparkling but irrelevant for it meant men like Cluny were not to hand as Cumberland marched on Inverness. On 12 April he crossed the Spey, unopposed because of the superior range of his artillery. When the Royal Navy deprived Charles of a shipment of French gold late in March, it doomed him to battle in April, before his army disintegrated. An attempt to mount a surprise night attack with half-starved troops against a

[In the collection of Macleod of Macleod, Dunvegan Castle, Isle of Skye]

Norman Macleod of Macleod, whose failure to join the '45 was a major blow to Prince Charles

watchful Hanoverian camp proved abortive, and on Wednesday 16 April 1746 the Jacobites returned to Culloden — Charles's chosen battlefield.

It was a crazy choice, made for him by his incompetent Adjutant-General, John O'Sullivan. Lord George Murray and all other competent observers saw what any visitor to the National Trust site now sees — a shooting range, flat and open, with low hills on one side, dykes on another. Its Gaelic name means Yellow Bog, so it was difficult even to mount a general attack across it. This was the first battle in which Charles truly commanded, and he showed as little military talent as he had hitherto shown political understanding. His strength of character derived from a totally self-centred conviction that God was on his side and that 'his' subjects would never seriously resist him in the name of a usurper. Facing an army of 9,000 well-fed and disciplined men with half their number of starving Highland peasants, he expected to win. Belford's guns first outclassed his own, and then started to blow his ragged ranks apart. Still Charles did not get the message. A charge would solve all.

A charge went in, involving the Jacobite centre and right wing. Led by the Clan Chattan regiment with the yellow-haired MacGillivray of Dunmaglass out in front with his standard-bearer, it was pressed with incredible heroism, and backed by reinforcements brought up by Lord George Murray. A hail of musketry and case-shot decimated and disordered the attackers before they hit the triple ranks of bayonets which proved more lethal than broadswords. Perhaps 1,500 clansmen charged home, climbing over their own dead to attack. Lochiel fell wounded in both ankles. Barrel's and Munro's Regiments split apart but kept fighting the Jacobites until Sempill's Regiment could deliver the Hanoverian counter-attack. In half an hour the issue was decided. The Hanoverian line began to move forward. The Jacobite right refused to go on the offensive, not unreasonably, for another charge would simply have doubled casualties. Now Hanoverian horse and Campbell militia moved in for the kill on the dissolving Jacobite ranks, and the professional French troops (sure of being treated as prisoners of war if captured) moved into the standard defensive routines designed to slow down pursuing cavalry while Charles was led off the field. Reality had finally caught up with him.

CHAPTER VIII

After the '45

MORALE IN THE JACOBITE ARMY HAD BEEN VERY LOW
on the morning of Culloden. When Lord Elcho then asked Lord
George Murray what he thought the outlook was, the reply had
been 'We are putting an end to a bad affair'. Lord Kilmarnock had
been equally depressed. Before being executed for high treason in
1746 he explained that 'for the two kings and their rights, I cared not
a farthing . . . but I was starving, and . . . if Mahommed had set up his
standard in the Highlands I had . . . stuck close to the party, for I
must eat'. These remarks, though a salutary reminder that not
everyone in the eighteenth century accepted officially-approved
values, were not typical of the upper-class participants in the rising.
Most of them were convinced Jacobites, but they had come to have
grave reservations about the behaviour of Prince Charles. Jacobite
ideology was a conservative critique of Hanoverian Britain, and a set
of moral, political and religious values. It was not a promissory note
which could arbitrarily be cashed on demand. Neither James VII and
II, nor the Old Pretender, had ever dreamed of landing in Britain
unless they had French troops with them, or an established rebellion to join. Charles alone of his family had simply arrived and
demanded total commitment. Many men of Jacobite convictions
had hung back or prevaricated. The wily Lovat is a prime example,
though he had come off the fence at the very last moment, and he
lost his head for this, one of the few unequivocal acts of his career.
The elder Allan Ramsay, hairdresser, poet, theatrical entrepreneur
and Jacobite, thoughtfully went off for a holiday when Prince
Charles occupied Edinburgh. Behind most of the unease even in Jacobite circles lay the view which Lord George Murray expressed in a
passionately angry letter he wrote to Charles immediately after
Culloden, in which he said:

'It was surely wrong to set up the Royal Standard without

16. *Prince Charles Edward Stewart, the Young Pretender, as a boy
(from a painting by Antonio David, 1732)*

17. *Prince Charles as a disappointed middle-aged man*
    (from a painting attributed to Hugh Douglas Hamilton)

having positive assurance from his most Christian Majesty that he would assist you with all his might.'

By the time he penned these lines, which Charles never forgave, Lord George was an embittered man. He knew Culloden was a battle which should never have been fought. He thought the correct military strategy for the Jacobites in the spring of 1746 would have been a guerrilla campaign in the central Highlands, for which supplies and munitions would have had to have been moved inland from Inverness long before the start of April. Like most members of the Jacobite army, he was shocked by the failure of Prince Charles to appoint any rendezvous for his men in the event of defeat. After Culloden a high proportion of the Jacobites still under arms did meet at Ruthven in Badenoch, and they were surprisingly full of fight. Again, they were shocked to receive a message from Charles telling each man to make his own way to safety as best he could, nor was the blow softened by the news that the Prince had taken most available funds with him to assist his own flight through a starving countryside. Jacobitism stressed the patriarchal, the fatherly status of kingship. Sub jects were not mere tools, they were children. The raw egotism of Charles, and his bland indifference to the appalling price his devoted followers were paying for his ambitions sat ill to his own creed.

Yet the French were indeed the key, not only to recent events, but also to the future. The '45 underlined the unacceptable level of risk involved in a rising which did not enjoy substantial French military aid. The Jacobite high command knew that Charles had misled them about French commitment. They were also profoundly disillusioned with the English Tories. On 9 October 1745 Charles had issued a proclamation declaring that all those who attended 'the Elector of Hanover's' Parliament, summoned for 17 October at Westminster would be deemed guilty of 'an overt Act of Treason and Rebellion'. Tory MPs practically tripped over one another to get to Westminster. None of the leading Jacobite commanders was ever likely to believe Charles again on the subject of French or Tory pledges. Some of the wisest of the exiled Jacobite leadership, such as the Earl Marischal, had always been opposed to what he regarded as the irresponsible escapade of the '45. By 1759 he had come to terms with George II and was one of the first forfeited Jacobites to buy his estate back, though it is clear he never abandoned his basic hostility to the Act of Union of 1707.

Humbler Jacobites kept their faith in the charismatic personality of Prince Charles. Had this not been so, he would not have been able to survive as a hunted fugitive in the Highlands between April and early September 1746, when Antoine Walsh, to his credit, finally succeeded in bringing him off safely from Loch nan Uamh after several increasingly desperate rescue attempts. Even people like Flora MacDonald, herself no Jacobite, felt that it was her duty as a Highland lady to assist the escape of a hunted prince of Scotland's ancient dynasty (in her case by allowing him to travel in her entourage, disguised as her maidservant). What really killed any serious prospect of another Jacobite rebellion in the Highlands was the widespread conviction amongst Highlanders after Culloden that they had been betrayed by the French. In fact they had not been betrayed. Louis XV himself had been quite keen on re-activating invasion plans, but French policy was determined by debate in committees, and the key committees never agreed to reinstate the invasion as a first priority. De Saxe, the best and best-informed of contemporary French generals, argued passionately against such a decision because it could not guarantee even to land its expeditionary force, but assembling that force was guaranteed to strip him of the numerical superiority which was underpinning his successes in Flanders.

When British and French armies faced one another on the Heights of Abraham outside Quebec in 1759, to battle for the destiny of Canada, the aide-de-camp to the French commander Montcalm was a Scots Jacobite. In the British army of General Wolfe (himself a Hanoverian officer at Culloden) were other Scots Jacobites who regarded this battle as a chance to be revenged for French treachery during the '45. Their view was irrational, but not entirely misguided. The French emissary to Prince Charles had privately advised his government, after all hope was lost, that it might be more fun, and more profitable, to run the next Scotish rebellion on a republican basis. Nothing would have suited France better than an unsuccessful Scottish rebellion every four to five years. There was a bottomless cynicism in the execution of the foreign policy of His Most Christian Majesty which Scotsmen sensed.

That feeling was more decisive than all the brutality which rightly stained the name of Cumberland. There was first the butchery of the Jacobite wounded on the field of Culloden. Then there was his devastating sweep down the line of the Great Glen wreaking havoc as he went. Hanoverian troops burned houses and stole effects and cattle with absolutely no distinction between rebels and non-rebels. The very ambiguous behaviour of John MacDonell of Glengarry did nothing to shield his estates from being plundered. In a countryside near starvation, the destruction of the material basis of life was ultimately more punishing to the community than the many specific episodes of murder and rape. Locheil, who despite his wounds had actually tried to organise resistance to Cumberland's advance, had to accept in the end that resistance was impractical. He could not find meal to feed his men. The Camerons killed as many of their cattle as they could eat or salt down. The silver and other valuables from their chief's great wooden house at Achnacarry were buried for safety, but Lochiel had to watch the house go up in flames as troops ravaged his lands. No British government had hitherto been sufficiently interested in the Highlands to make a military effort big enough to destroy their ancient autonomy. Prince Charles had at least achieved the feat of bringing a large regular army into the heart of the Highlands, where its swathe of destruction was matched by equally savage amphibious operations conducted by the Royal Navy on the western seaboard.

Cumberland could not return to Flanders fast enough. He was succeeded in command in Scotland by his friend William Anne, second Earl of Albermarle, who was himself most anxious to leave what he regarded as a barbarous countryside for the Great Game of European power-politics. Albermarle testified, again and again, in official despatches, that all the punitive actions and collective punishments inflicted on the Jacobite clans seemed to have bred little else except defiance. Their spirit was not broken. That is one reason why a massive programme of military fortification was embarked on, to deal with the next rebellion. Fort William was strengthened, and Fort Augustus rebuilt, but old Fort George in Inverness was, correctly, judged inherently indefensible. At the suggestion of the town council a new site was found nine miles east of Inverness on the peninsula of Ardersier, where between 1748 and 1769 the most advanced and sophisticated bastion-defended artillery fort in all Europe was laid out on a huge scale, and with appropriate neo-classical embellishment. It proved a white elephant, for it has never heard a shot fired in anger. Contemporaries could only see the stubborn defiance of persecuted Highland peasants. Few could appreciate the revolution in the minds of the Highland aristocracy which made another '45 unthinkable.

The government produced a whole barrage of measures designed to destroy the culture and social structure of the Gaelic Highlands. Anything which made the Highlands different was regarded as a seedbed of Jacobitism. Highland dress was made illegal, though enforcement of the measure proved difficult and influential Whigs who happened to be Highlanders often ignored it, as their portraits show. Lowland Scots and English attitudes towards the Gaelic tongue were at best unenlightened. The '45, the last of a series of traumatic Highland descents into Lowland politics which had lasted nearly a century, raised hostility to Gaelic to fever pitch. It was to be stamped out, as a mark of incivility. Actually the state lacked the power to do this when it did not control a compulsory and universal education system. Although Gaelic did recede in linguistically mixed and unstable areas like easter Ross north of Inverness, it required the impact of compulsory education after 1872 to deal a death-blow to the Gaelic language on the mainland of Scotland. A hundred years of attrition after 1872 left it the everyday language of extensive areas only in the Hebrides.

What could be done by the stroke of a legislative pen was to abolish the network of private courts in aristocratic hands known as the heritable jurisdictions. This was done by 'An Act for taking away and abolishing the Heritable Jurisdictions in that part of Great Britain called Scotland, and for making satisfaction to the Proprietors thereof . . . and for rendering the Union of the Two Kingdoms more complete' (technically referred to as 20 Geo II. Cap. 43, 1747). The exercise was not quite as straightforward as was expected. In the first place, heritable jurisdictions were common in the Lowlands, and many were held by arch Whigs like Argyll or Sir Andrew Agnew of Lochnaw. The Agnews of Lochnaw were hereditary sheriffs of Galloway, and Sir Andrew, a peppery gentleman known as 'the peerless knight', had successfully defended Blair Castle against no less a Jacobite than Lord George Murray in March 1746. Furthermore, Duncan Forbes of Culloden, who had earned the epithet of 'old woman' from Cumberland for urging that royal brute to show clemency in his hour of victory, argued strongly against the abolition of baron courts. These feudal courts of first instance offered cheap local justice, and were important to landlords as a means of enforcing payment of rent. In the end they had to be retained, with reduced jurisdiction. All other hereditary jurisdictions were abolished, though with substantial compensation in money to the holders. At local level Scotland had at last, for weal or woe, left the Middle Ages behind.

The immediate effect of all these traumas on law and order in the Highlands appears to have been counter-productive. The central government could not provide efficient, cheap, acceptable forms of social discipline comparable to those which had evolved within traditional Gaelic society. It proved necessary to deploy regular troops in scattered outposts to act not as battle groups for the suppression of rebellion, but as a rural gendarmerie for the suppression of cattle stealing, illicit distilling, and smuggling. Existing forts such as Ruthven in Badenoch, Bernera near Glenelg, and Inversnaid beside Loch Lomond in Stirlingshire were used for this purpose. Around 1749 Inversnaid and Ruthven were both surrounded by a regular star-shaped curtain wall and about the same time the two native tower-houses of Corgarff at the head of the Don Valley and Braemar on Deeside were commandeered for garrison posts, and protected in the same fashion.

Corgarff, situated beside Cock Bridge at the foot of the very severe Lecht Road, is a fine example of this kind of post. A plain tower built around 1600 commanded the passes of the Dee, the Avon and the Don. It was remodelled and surrounded by a zigzag wall looped for musketry defence. Garrisoned from 1748 to 1802, it seems to have been deserted for a generation thereafter. Then in 1827-31 it was regarrisoned, as was Braemar Castle, by a captain, a subaltern, and fifty-six soldiers, in order to crush a revival of smug-gling in Strathdon. Slowly, very slowly, the Highlands acquired the habit of deference to alien authority.

Probably the numbing apathy bred by sustained economic col-lapse and depopulation in the nineteeth century was as important as any other factor in the creation of an obedient region, for the social engineering attempted by Hanoverian governments after the '45 was not conspicuously successful, even where it seemed to have great scope for action, as in the case of the forfeited Jacobite estates. As part of its policy of firm punishment and reform, the government forced through effective forfeiture of the estates of convicted rebels. These estates were first managed by the Barons of the Exchequer, and then in 1752 an Annexing Act turned thirteen of the estates into 'unalienably' annexed crown lands, managed by a board of honorary commissioners. As late as 1750 the Duke of Newcastle was receiving intelligence reports declaring that 'Highlanders seem more inclined to rebellion than ever'. The reports confused a lack of the docility regarded as a desirable characteristic of British subjects with will-ingness to raise a formal Jacobite rebellion, but they help explain why the government was prepared to devote all the profits of the estates to the task of eradicating Popery and Jacobitism, and to the propagation of Protestantism, loyalty to the Hanoverian dynasty, and habits of industry. In practice, the commissioners were benign landlords, most of whose positive schemes came to nothing. Geol-ogy and the climate alone ensured that Highland properties could not easily be turned into carbon copies of the fertile Lowlands. An attempt in the 1760s to establish Saxon civilisation by planting village colonies of discharged soldiers and sailors on the forfeited annexed estates proved hilariously unsuccessful. It did help the growth of the already established small town of Callander, but elsewhere it tended to underline the fact that what old sweats and tars acquired after years of brutalising service tended to be an aversion to honest work and a passion for hard liquor.

Abroad, Charles Edward Stuart at first showed his usual combination of energy and inability to see difficulties. He tried to use his popularity in France to embarrass the French government into committing 20,000 troops to his cause. Louis XV was more evasive even than normal, and eventually had Charles deported. By the early 1750s Charles had grasped, too late, the central problem of his dynasty's alienation from the Church of England, and went through a phase of reconciliation with it. A further complex of intrigues known rather innacurately as the Elibank plot was penetrated by the British government and cost the life of a gallant Jacobite gentleman, Dr Archibald Cameron, who had left Scotland with Charles in 1746, but who was captured and executed in 1753. Frederick the Great, arguably the most cynical of all crypto-Jacobites, had toyed with these intrigues as a means of vexing the Elector of Hanover.

After 1754 Charles went into a definite physical and moral decline and his public reputation was ruined by reports of his excessive drinking. In 1760 his Scottish mistress Clementina Walkinshaw left him, taking with her their daughter Charlotte. Succession to his father's titles on the death of that tired old man in 1766, did not even stimulate Charles to issue the usual commemorative medallion, though his bother Henry, who had enraged Charles by accepting a cardinal's hat in 1747 had the Italian sculptor Fillipo Cropanese produce one of himself. The late 1760s saw Charles come under the sensible influence of a new secretary of state John Caryll, who negotiated his marriage with a minor German princess, Louisa of Stolberg-Gedern. The French, anxious for the procreation of a handy supply of Stuart pretenders, paid for the dowry, though their own last serious plan for an invasion of Britain on a Jacobite basis had foundered with the defeat of their Atlantic fleet in the battle of Quiberon Bay in 1759.

For a year or two Louisa was a political asset. Then the marriage began to sink. In 1775 Charles sacked Caryll. In 1780 a more than usually violent St Andrew's Day binge by Charles made his wife leave her alcoholic spouse, first for a convent, then for her lover

Alfieri. Formal separation was acknowledged in 1784, when Charles re-activated his relationship with his daughter Charlotte, whom he legitimised as Duchess of Albany. She nursed him through to death in January 1788.

Jacobitism as a cause was dead. Even the non-juring Scots Episcopalians agreed to pray for George III after 1788. By then the Jacobite aristocracy of the Highlands had engineered its reconciliation with the Hanoverian regime, mainly by raising regiments for overseas service for the British army. The idea that Culloden was immediately followed by the Clearances which drove the Highland people off their ancient lands is rubbish. There was a long period when Highland landlords wanted hands, for recruiting purposes, and for the kelp industry which made industrial alkali by burning seaweed. Lovat's son, Simon Fraser, a reluctant Jacobite colonel at Culloden, pioneered the technique of trading recruits for political favour. He and his regiment of Fraser's Highlanders were with Wolfe at Quebec. The Seven Years War, known in America as the French and Indian War, saw the principle of raising regiments in ex-Jacobite areas accepted, indeed gloried in by so eminent a war minister as the Elder William Pitt. Simon Fraser had his estates restored in 1774. All the other forfeited estates were returned in 1784 by a piece of legislation which lauded the massive efforts of the former Jacobite families to assist the Crown in the recently lost War of American Independence.

'King Henry IX', the former Duke of York in the Jacobite succession, had the good sense not to take his nineteen-year 'reign' very seriously. Charlotte, Duchess of Albany had started to sell relics of the Stuart martyr-king Charles I to the British government immediately after her father's death. Henry issued only one medal, bearing the inscription Henry IX 'Non desideriis hominum sed voluntate Dei' (not by the wishes of men but by the will of God) but it was really a reissue of his 1766 medal, and he usually gave it away to visitors, including the banker Thomas Coutts, who took one back to George III. After French armies invaded Italy and seized his estates, Henry became a pensioner of George III, and the Jacobite archives became the last Stuart relics sold to the Hanoverian family.

The authoritarian, absolutist side of the Jacobite tradition did not die. It was transferred to the ideology of the Westminster-based political system of Hanoverian Britain only too successfully by High Churchmen, and by nostalgic reactionaries like Dr Johnson, a neo-Jacobite pensioner of George III, like 'Henry IX'. In that sense, the transfer of Jacobite relics and archives was appropriate. It is no accident that amongst the bitterest enemies of the American patriots in the 1770s were a clutch of men with a neo-Jacobite background, like Johnson, Allan Ramsay the painter son and namesake of the prudent Scots barber-poet of the '45, and above all William Murray Earl of Mansfield, whose early letters in the Stuart archives show him indeed to have been the committed Jacobite he spent the rest of his highly successful political life denying he had ever been. Recent Highland emigrants to America tended, when war broke out in 1775, to rally behind their aristocratic leaders, and behind the King's government.

On the other hand, Jacobites who had left for America soon after the '15 or the '45, or their descendants, were just as likely to be American Patriots and enemies of Westminster in 1775. There is no inconsistency in this, for they represented the other side of the Jacobite coin, or perhaps one should say medal: the 'Country' side. As a protest against the betrayal of 'Revolution Principles', and more particularly against an over-centralised government over-dominated by an increasingly irresponsible executive 'managing', or as critics preferred to say 'corrupting', the legislature, the 'Country' tradition was the main vehicle for active opposition to the Westminster regime. Virtually all Americans embraced it, and though only a minority of 'Country' opponents of government were Jacobite, nearly all active British Jacobites were 'Country' in their views. In the last analysis, Jacobitism made a major contribution to the ultimate failure of the 'Country' tradition in Britain in the eighteenth century. The 'Court' Whigs had some bad moments as a few enterprising Scottish gentlemen at the head of the half-starved peasantry of the Grampian Highlands whipped the grossly inadequate home defence forces of Hanoverian Britain again and again; but nothing strengthens abuses more than unsuccessful protests against them. The social and religious world of Jacobitism is gone beyond recall. In that sense it is dead as a positive creed. What Jacobites protested against is, however, only too often alive. Some of the issues which excited Lord George Murray, Lovat, or the Jacobite Earl Marischal are more pressing than ever. Such men must not be consigned to some Jacobite Valhalla. We shall not see their like again, but we owe it to them to recognise that they, like us, wrestled with timeless problems of the relationship between government and its subjects.

Properties of the National Trust for Scotland which have connections with the Jacobite period

Castle Fraser *(off B993, 3 m S of Kemnay, 16 m W of Aberdeen)*

One of the Castles of Mar, a 16th-century tower house, extended in the early 17th, perhaps the finest example of its kind. Charles, IV Lord Fraser, was an active Jacobite in 1715 and was killed by a fall over a Banffshire cliff whilst a fugitive after the Rising.

Craigievar *(on A980, 6 m S of Alford, 26 m W of Aberdeen)*

A splendid example of the Scottish tower house, completed in 1626 for a Forbes laird, 'Willie the Merchant', who made his money in the Baltic trade. Of Craigievar Stewart Cruden said, 'it claims a Scottish place in the front rank of European Architecture.'

Culloden *(on B9006, 5 m E of Inverness)*

The site of the battle between Prince Charles and the Duke of Cumberland on 16 April 1746, which ended Jacobite hopes for ever. Old Leanach Cottage furnished in the style of that time and Visitor Centre. Recent clearance of woods brings out the appalling exposure of the Jacobite line to superior Hanoverian artillery.

Dunkeld *(off A9, 15 m N of Perth)*

Small town whose centre has now been beautifully restored by the Trust. It saw vicious street fighting in 1689, after the rout of King William's troops by the Jacobites at Killiecrankie. Claverhouses's death in that battle was followed by the defeat of his men at Dunkeld, where Williamite forces blocked their bid to reach the Lowlands.

Fyvie Castle   *(off A947, 8 m SE of Turriff, 25 m NW of Aberdeen)*

This magnificent castle was the forfeited seat of the Jacobite Setons of Fyvie, Earls of Dunfermline. Sir Herbert Maxwell called it 'the crowning glory of Scottish baronial architecture'.

Glencoe   *(A82)*

Scene of the Massacre in 1692 when Campbell of Glenlyon and 128 of his men treacherously turned on their hosts, killing about 40 of them. The Glen has some of Scotland's most dramatic mountain scenery. The Trust acquired 14,200 acres of the Glen in 1937, including the main MacDonald settlement areas and Bidean nam Bian, the highest mountain in Argyll. Visitor Centre.

Glenfinnan Monument   *(A830, 18½ m W of Fort William)*

Marks the place on the shores of Loch Shiel where Prince Charles Edward raised his Standard on 19 August 1745. The monument was erected in 1815 by a descendant of one of the men 'out' at the start of the '45. There is a Trust shop by the roadside.

Hill of Tarvit   *(off A916, 2½ m S of Cupar, Fife)*

A mansion dating from 1696 was virtually rebuilt by Sir Robert Lorimer in 1906, to house the art collection of Mr F.B. Sharp. It replaced the original tower house, **Scotstarvit**, ¾ of a mile to the West, which was the seat of the Royalist writer Sir John Scot, author of *The Staggering State of Scots Statesmen Revealed.*

House of Dun   *(on A935, 4 m W of Montrose)*

Though the present building is largely to the designs of William Adam, original plans were drawn up by 'Bobbing Johnnie' Erskine, Earl of Mar and leader of the '15.

Kellie Castle   *(on B9171, 3 m NNW of Pittenweem, Fife)*

A medieval castle, extended in the 16th and early 17th centuries. The Earls of Kellie eventually sought solace from unsuccessful Jacobite politics in music. In the late 19th and early 20th century Kellie was the home of Robert Lorimer, one of the great restorers of Scottish vernacular architecture.

Kintail   *(N of A87, 16 m E of Kyle of Lochalsh)*

Beautiful area of West Highland scenery, including the Five Sisters of Kintail, the scene of the Rising of 1719. The Trust property here is on the site of a Clan Macrae settlement. The Macraes were known as 'Mackenzie's shirt of mail' for their military service to the Chief of Clan Mackenzie, later the Earl of Seaforth. Seaforth was 'out' in the '15 and the '19, but not in the '45.

Pass of Killiecrankie   *(off A9, 3 m N of Pitlochry)*

Scene of the battle on 27 July 1689 where the Jacobite General Graham of Claverhouse was killed in the hour of victory over General Mackay's Government troops. The battle was fought not in the Pass but higher up, about 1 m N near Urrard House. The Soldier's Leap over the River Garry is said to have been jumped by Donald MacBean, of the fleeing Williamite forces.

Scotstarvit Tower *see* **Hill of Tarvit**

Stirling Castle (not a Trust property)

The strategic pivot of Scotland. The Castle was unsuccessfully besieged by Prince Charles's army during the '45 Rising. *The Visitor Centre is now run by the Trust.*

Index

Numbers in *italics* indicate illustrations

*Line illustrations on pages 25, 26 and 106 are by John Marshall
Map on page 6 by Regmarad*

*For permission to published illustrations
we are grateful to the following:
The National Trust for Scotland
The National Galleries of Scotland
The Royal Museum of Scotland*